FEMA 182/August 1989

I0500581

Landslide Loss Reduction:
A Guide for State and Local Government Planning

EARTHQUAKE HAZARDS REDUCTION SERIES 52

Issued by FEMA in furtherance of the Decade for Natural Disaster Reduction.

Landslide Loss Reduction:
A Guide for State and Local Government Planning

by:
Robert L. Wold, Jr.
Colorado Division of Disaster Emergency Services
and
Candace L. Jochim
Colorado Geological Survey

Contents

Contents Continued

Figures

Tables

Foreword

There is a need for a comprehensive program to reduce landslide losses in the United States that marshals the capability of all levels of government and the private sector. Without such a program, the heavy and widespread losses to the nation and to individuals from landslides will increase greatly. Successful and cost-effective landslide loss-reduction actions can and should be taken in the many jurisdictions facing landslide problems. The responsibility for dealing with landslides principally falls upon state and local governments and the private sector. The federal government can provide research, technical guidance, and limited funding assistance, but to meet their responsibility for maintaining the public's health, safety and welfare, state and local governments must prevent and reduce landslide losses through hazard mapping, land-use management, and building and grading controls. In partnership with public interest groups and governments, the private sector must also increase its efforts to reduce landslide hazards.

Dramatic landslide loss reduction can be achieved. The effective use of landslide building codes and grading ordinances by a few state and local governments in the nation clearly demonstrates that successful programs can be put into place with reasonable costs. Numerous examples of responsible landslide hazard planning and mitigation by private developers exist but are usually overshadowed by improper development that ignores the hazard.

Transfer of proven governmental and private sector landslide hazard mitigation techniques to other jurisdictions throughout the nation is one of the most effective ways of helping to reduce future landslide losses. This guide, prepared by the State of Colorado for the Federal Emergency Management Agency, builds upon the impressive efforts taken by Colorado state and local governments in planning for and mitigating landslide losses. The Federal Emergency Management Agency hopes that this guide and the accompanying plan for landslide hazard mitigation will stimulate and assist other state and local governments, private interests, and citizens throughout the nation to reduce the landslide threat.

Arthur J. Zeizel
Project Officer
Federal Emergency
    Management Agency

Acknowledgments

This project was funded in part by the Federal Emergency Management Agency (FEMA), the Colorado Division of Disaster Emergency Services (DODES), the Colorado Geological Survey (CGS), and the U.S. Geological Survey (Grant No. 14–08–0001–A0420).

The document was written and prepared by **Robert L. Wold, Jr.** (DODES) and **Candace L. Jochim** (CGS). Staff contributors included: **William P. Rogers**, **Irwin M. Glassman**, and **John O. Truby**. Additional contributors included: **David B. Prior** of the Coastal Studies Institute of Louisiana State University and **William J. Kockelman** of the U.S. Geological Survey. Project management was provided by **Arthur Zeizel** (FEMA) and **Irwin Glassman** (DODES).

Other essential project personnel included: **Cheryl Brchan** (drafting and layout), **Nora Rimando** (word processing), and **David Butler** (editing).

Advisory Committee

John Beaulieu, *Deputy State Geologist, Oregon*

John P. Byrne, *Director, Disaster Emergency Services, Colorado*

William J. Kockelman, *Planner, U.S. Geological Survey, California*

Peter Lessing, *Environmental Geologist, West Virginia Geological Survey*

George Mader, *President, William Spangle and Associates, California*

Dr. Robert L. Schuster, *U.S. Geological Survey, Colorado*

Dr. James E. Slosson, *Chief Engineering Geologist, Slosson and Associates, California*

Darrell Waller, *State Coordinator, Bureau of Disaster Services, Idaho*

According to available information, landsliding in the United States causes an average of 25 to 50 deaths (Committee on Ground Failure Hazards, 1985) and $1 to $2 billion in economic losses annually (Schuster and Fleming, 1986). Although all 50 states are subject to landslide activity, the Rocky Mountain, Appalachian, and Pacific Coast regions generally suffer the greatest landslide losses (Figures 1a, b). The costs of landsliding can be direct or indirect and range from the expense of cleanup and repair or replacement of structures to lost tax revenues and reduced productivity and property values.

Landslide losses are growing in the United States despite the availability of successful techniques for landslide management and control. The failure to lessen the problem is primarily due to the ever-increasing pressure of development in areas of geologically hazardous terrain and the failure of responsible government entities and private developers to recognize landslide hazards and to apply appropriate measures for their mitigation, even though there is overwhelming evidence that landslide hazard mitigation programs serve both public and private interests by saving many times the cost of implementation. The high cost of landslide damage (Table 1) will continue to increase if community development and capital investments continue without taking advantage of the opportunities that currently exist to mitigate the effects of landslides.

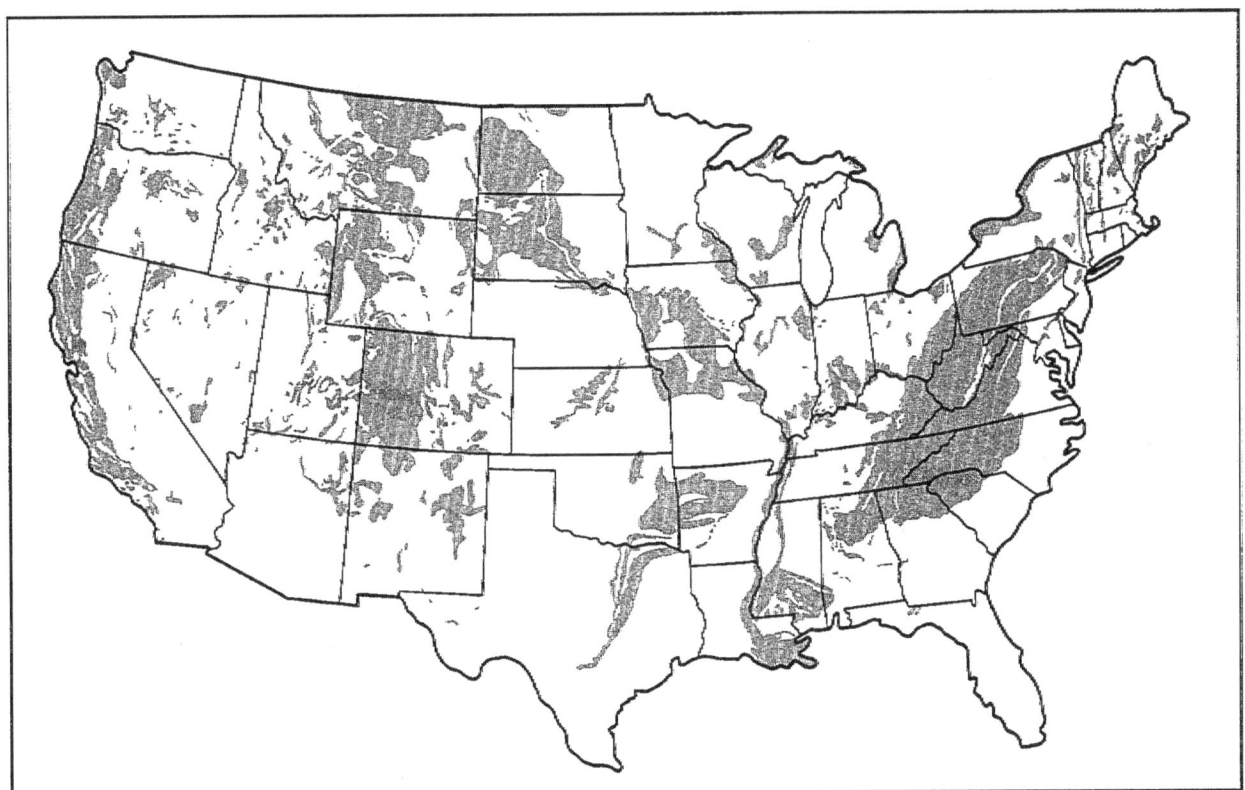

Figure 1a. Map showing relative potential of different parts of the conterminous United States to landsliding (U.S. Geological Survey, 1981a).

| State | Damage 1973–1983 | | | |
	State Roads ($M)	Priv. Prop. ($M)	Total ($M)	Ann. Avg. ($M)
Alabama	10.0	0.5	10.5	1.05
Alaska	10.0	0.0	10.0	1.0
Arizona	2.0	0.0	2.0	0.2
Arkansas	2.0	0.0	2.0	0.2
California	800.0 ?	200.0 ?	1000.0 ?	100.0 ?
Colorado	20.0	50.0	70.0	7.0
Connecticut	0.0	0.0	0.0	0.0
Delaware	2.0	0.0	2.0	0.2
Dist. of Columbia	0.1	0.1	0.01	0.8
Florida	0.0	0.0	0.0	0.0
Georgia	1.0 ?	0.0	1.0 ?	0.1 ?
Hawaii	4.0	0.5	4.5	0.45
Idaho	10.0 ?	1.0 ?	11.0 ?	1.1 ?
Illinois	1.0	1.0 ?	2.0 ?	0.2 ?
Indiana	10.0	1.0	11.0	1.1
Iowa	1.0	0.3	1.3	0.13
Kansas	1.0	0.3 ?	1.3 ?	0.13
Kentucky	180.0	10.0 ?	190.0 ?	19.0 ?
Louisiana	2.0	0.3	2.3	0.23
Maine	0.3	0.3	0.6	0.06
Maryland	20.0	0.0	20.0	2.0
Massachusetts	0.3	0.0	0.3	0.03
Michigan	0.1	0.0	0.1	0.01
Minnesota	7.0	0.0	7.0	0.7
Mississippi	3.0	0.5	3.5	0.35
Missouri	2.0 ?	1.0 ?	3.0 ?	0.3 ?
Montana	10.0 ?	1.0 ?	11.0 ?	1.1 ?
Nebraska	0.4	0.4 ?	0.8 ?	0.08 ?
Nevada	2.0 ?	0.5	2.5 ?	0.25 ?
New Hampshire	10.0	0.0	10.0	1.0
New Jersey	3.0	3.0	6.0	0.6
New Mexico	3.0	1.0	4.0	0.4
New York	20.0	50.0 ?	70.0 ?	7.0 ?
North Carolina	45.0	0.5	45.5	4.55
North Dakota	4.0	0.0	4.0	0.4
Ohio	60.0 ?	40.0	100.0 ?	10.0
Oklahoma	2.0 ?	0.0	2.0 ?	0.2 ?
Oregon	30.0	10.0	40.0	4.0
Pennsylvania	50.0	10.0 ?	60.0 ?	6.0
Rhode Island	0.0	0.0	0.0	0.0
South Carolina	0.0	0.0	0.0	0.0
South Dakota	16.0	2.0	18.0	1.8
Tennessee	100.0	10.0 ?	110.0 ?	11.0 ?
Texas	8.0	0.0	8.0	0.8
Utah	200.0 ?	10.0 ?	210.0 ?	21.0 ?
Vermont	3.0	0.5	3.5	0.35
Virginia	11.0	1.0	12.0	1.2
Washington	70.0 ?	30.0 ?	100.0 ?	10.0 ?
West Virginia	270.0	5.0	275.0	27.5
Wisconsin	0.2	0.5	0.7	0.07
Wyoming	4.0	0.0	4.0	0.4
Total (U.S.)	**2010.3**	**442.2**	**2452.5**	**245.25**

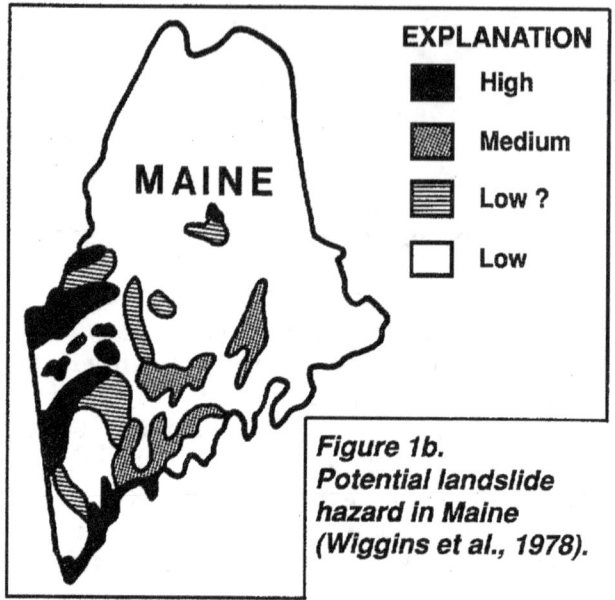

Figure 1b.
Potential landslide hazard in Maine (Wiggins et al., 1978).

The widespread occurrence of landsliding, together with the potential for catastrophic statewide and regional impacts, emphasizes the need for cooperation among federal, state, and local governments and the private sector. Although annual landslide losses in the U.S. are extremely high, significant reductions in future losses can be achieved through a combination of landslide hazard mitigation and emergency management.

Landslide hazard mitigation consists of those activities that reduce the likelihood of occurrence of damaging landslides and minimize the effects of the landslides that do occur. The goal of emergency management is to minimize loss of life and property damage through the timely and efficient commitment of available resources.

Despite their common goals, emergency management and hazard mitigation activities have historically been carried out independently. The integration of these two efforts is most often demonstrated in the recovery phase following a disaster, when decisions about reconstruction and future land uses in the community are made.

Emergency management, if well executed, can do much to minimize the loss and suffering associated with a particular disaster. However, unless it is guided by the goals of preventing or reducing long-term hazard losses, it is unlikely to reduce the adverse impact of future disasters significantly. This is where mitigation becomes important (Advisory Board on the Built Environment, 1983, p. 9).

Purpose of this Guidebook

As mentioned above, the development and implementation of landslide loss-reduction strategies requires the cooperation of many public and private institutions, all levels of government, and private citizens. Coordinated and comprehensive systems for landslide hazard mitigation do not currently exist in most states and communities faced with the problem. In most states, local governments often take the lead by identifying goals and objectives, controlling land use, providing hazard information and technical assistance to property owners and developers, and implementing mitigation projects as resources allow. State and federal agencies play supporting roles—primarily financial, technical, and administrative. In some cases, however, legislation originating at the state or federal level is the sole impetus for stimulating effective local mitigation activity.

In many states there remains a need to develop long-term organizational systems at state and local levels to deal with landslide hazard mitigation in a coordinated and systematic manner. The development of a landslide hazard mitigation plan can be the initial step in the establishment of state and local programs that promote long-term landslide loss reduction.

The purpose of this guidebook is to provide a practical, politically feasible guide for state and local officials involved in landslide hazard mitigation. The guidebook presents concepts and a framework for the preparation of state and local landslide hazard mitigation plans. It outlines a basic methodology, provides information on available resources, and offers suggestions on the formation of an interdisciplinary mitigation planning team and a permanent state natural hazards mitigation organization. Individual states and local jurisdictions can adapt the suggestions in this book to meet their own unique needs.

Because of its involvement in identifying and mitigating landslide hazards, the state of Colorado was selected by the Federal Emergency Management Agency (FEMA) to produce a prototype state landslide hazard mitigation plan. The technical information contained in the plan was designed to be transferable to other states and local jurisdictions and suitable for incorporation into other plans. The planning process can also serve as an example to other states and localities dealing with landslide problems. The materials contained in the Colorado Landslide Hazard Mitigation Plan (Colorado Geological Survey et al., 1988) were intended to complement the information presented in this guidebook. In an effort to promote landslide hazard mitigation nationally, FEMA has provided for the distribution of these two documents to all states. ❏

Chapter 2
Landslide Losses and the Benefits of Mitigation

The Landslide Hazard

Landsliding is a natural process which occurs and recurs in certain geologic settings under certain conditions. The rising costs of landslide damages are a direct consequence of the increasing vulnerability of people and structures to the hazard. In most regions, the overall rate of occurrence and severity of naturally caused landslides has not increased. What has increased is the extent of human occupation of these lands and the impact of human activities on the environment. Many landslide damages that have occurred might have been prevented or avoided if accurate landslide hazard information had been available and used.

Economic and Social Impacts of Landsliding

Costs of Landsliding

The most commonly cited figures on landslide losses are $1 to $2 billion in economic losses and 25 to 50 deaths annually. However, these figures are probably conservative because they were generated in the late 1970s. Since that time, the use of marginally suitable land has increased, as has inflation. Furthermore, there are no exhaustive compilations of landslide loss data for the United States, so these figures are basically extrapolations of the available data.

The high losses from landsliding are illustrated in Table 1. Surveys indicate that damage to private property accounts for 30 to 50 percent of the total costs (U.S. Geological Survey, 1982). Examples of costs associated with individual landslide events from representative areas across the country include:

ALASKA—It has been estimated (Youd, 1978) that 60 percent of the $300 million damage from the 1964 Alaska earthquake was the direct result of landslides.

CALIFORNIA—In 1982 in the San Francisco Bay Region, 616 mm (24.3 in.) of rain fell in 34 hours causing thousands of landslides which killed 25 people and caused more than $66 million in damage (Keefer et al., 1987).

TEXAS—In Dallas in the 1960s, a toppling failure occurred in a vertical exposure of a geological formation known as the Austin Chalk. This closed two lanes of a major downtown thoroughfare for eight months. Costs of construction of remedial measures and construction delays amounted to about $2.8 million (Allen and Flanigan, 1986).

UTAH—In 1983, a massive landslide dammed Spanish Fork Canyon, creating a lake. The landslide buried sections of the Denver and Rio Grande Western Railroad and U.S. Highways 6, 50, and 89 and inundated the town of Thistle. The estimated total losses and reconstruction costs due to this one landslide range from $200 million (University of Utah, Bureau of Economic and Business Research, 1984) to $600 million (Kaliser and Slosson, 1988).

WEST VIRGINIA—In 1975, landslide movements in colluvial soil damaged 56 houses in McMechen, West Virginia, located on a hillside above the Ohio River. This landslide was attributed to above normal precipitation. Mitigation was accomplished by grading and surface and subsurface drainage (Gray and Gardner, 1977).

Impacts and Consequences of Landsliding

Economic losses due to landsliding include both direct and indirect costs. Schuster and Fleming (1986) define direct costs as the costs of replacement, repair, or maintenance due to damage to property or facilities within the actual boundaries of a landslide (Figure 2). Such facilities include highways, railroads, irrigation canals, underwater communication cables, offshore oil platforms, pipelines, and dams. The cost of cleanup must also be included (Figure 3). All other landslide costs are considered to be indirect. Examples of indirect costs given by Schuster and Fleming (1986) include:

(1) reduced real estate values,
(2) loss of productivity of agricultural or forest lands,
(3) loss of tax revenues from properties devalued as a result of landslides,
(4) costs of measures to prevent or mitigate future landslide damage,
(5) adverse effects on water quality in streams,
(6) secondary physical effects, such as landslide-caused flooding, for which the costs are both direct and indirect,
(7) loss of human productivity due to injury or death.

Other examples are:

(8) fish kills,
(9) costs of litigation.

In addition to economic losses, there are intangible costs of landsliding such as personal stress, reduced quality of life, and the destruction of personal possessions having great sentimental value. Because costs of indirect and intangible losses are difficult or impossible to calculate, they are often undervalued or ignored. If they are taken into account, they often produce highly variable estimates of damage for a particular incident.

Figure 2. Major damage to homes in Farmington, Utah as a result of 1983 Rudd Creek mudslide (photograph by Robert Kistner, Kistner and Associates).

Figure 3. Local volunteers form "bucket brigade" to help clean mud and debris from homes in Farmington, Utah in 1983 (photograph by Robert Kistner, Kistner and Associates).

Long–Term Benefits of Mitigation

Studies have been conducted to estimate the potential savings when measures to minimize the effects of landsliding are applied. One early study by Alfors et al. (1973) attempted to forecast the potential costs of landslide hazards in California for the period 1970-2000 and the effects of applying mitigative measures. Under the conditions of applying all feasible measures at state-of-the-art levels (for the 1970s), there was a 90 percent reduction in losses for a benefit/cost ratio of 8.7:1, or $8.7 saved for every $1 spent. Nilsen and Turner (1975) estimated that approximately 80 percent of the landslides in Contra Costa County, California are related to human activity. In Allegheny County, Pennsylvania, 90 percent are related to such activity according to Briggs et al. (1975).

Because most landslides triggered by man are directly related to construction activities, appropriate grading codes can significantly decrease landslide losses in urban areas. Slosson (1969) compared landslide losses in Los Angeles for those sites constructed prior to 1952, when no grading codes existed and soils engineering and engineering geology were not required, with losses sustained at sites after such codes were enacted. He found that the monetary losses were reduced by approximately 97 percent.

The Cincinnati, Ohio Study

In 1985, the U.S. Geological Survey, in cooperation with the Federal Emergency Managament Agency, conducted a geologic/economic development study in the Cincinnati, Ohio area. This study developed a systematic approach to quantitative forecasting of probable landslide activity. Landslide probabilities derived from a reproducible procedure were combined with property value data to forecast the potential economic losses in scenarios for proposed development and to quantitatively identify the potential benefits of mitigation activities.

The study area was divided into 14,255 grid cells of 100-square meters each. Information calculated for each cell included: probability of landslide occurrence, economic loss in the event of a landslide, cost of mitigation, and economic benefit of mitigation. This information was used to develop a mitigation strategy. In areas where both slope and shear strength information were available, the optimum strategy required mitigation in those cells with slopes steeper than 14 degrees or where materials had effective residual stress friction angles of less than 26 degrees. This strategy yielded $1.7 million in estimated annualized net benefits for the community. In areas where only slope information was used, the best strategy required mitigation in those cells where slopes were greater than 8 degrees. This yielded an estimated annualized net benefit of $1.4 million. Therefore, using regional geologic information in addition to slope information resulted in an additional $300,000 net benefit. The Cincinnati study cost only $20,000 to prepare (Bernknopf et al., 1985).

The Benefits of Mitigation in Japan

Japan has what is considered by many to be the world's most comprehensive landslide loss reduction program. In 1958, the Japanese government enacted strong legislation that provided for land-use planning and the construction of check dams, drainage systems, and other physical controls to prevent landslides. The success of the program is indicated by the dramatic reduction in losses over time (Figure 4). In 1938, 130,000 homes were destroyed and more than 500 lives were lost due to landslides in the Kobe area. However, since the Japanese program went into effect, losses have decreased dramatically. In 1976—one of Japan's worst years for landsliding—only 2000 homes were destroyed with fewer than 125 lives lost (Schuster and Fleming, 1986).

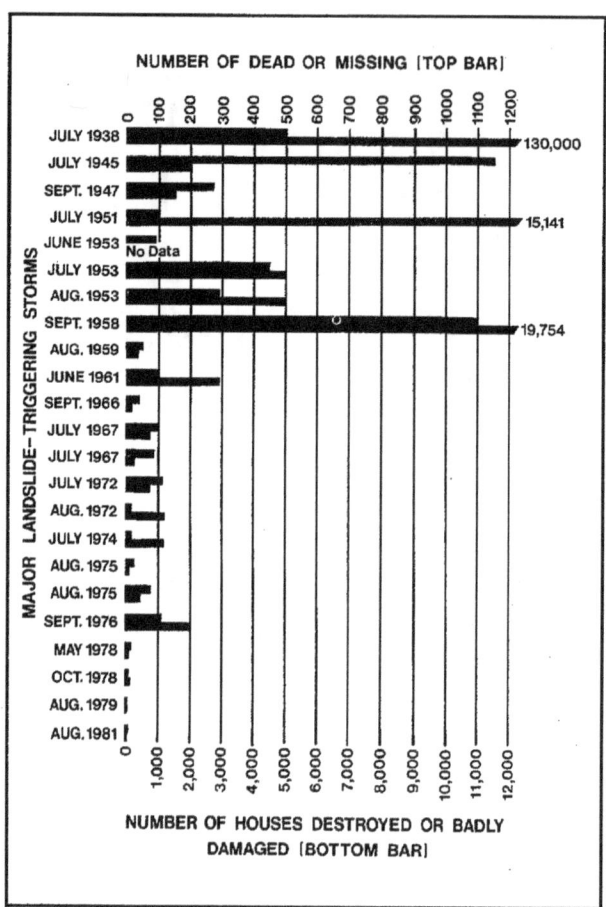

Figure 4. Losses due to major landslide disasters (mainly debris flows) in Japan from 1938–1981. All of these landslides were caused by heavy rainfall, most commonly related to typhoons, and many were associated with catastrophic flooding (data from Ministry of Construction, Japan, 1983).

Planning as a Means of Loss Reduction

The extent and severity of the landslide hazard in a particular area will determine the need for a landslide hazard mitigation plan.

Communities that have landslide problems are encouraged to assess the costs of damage to public and private property and weigh those costs against the costs of a landslide reduction program. The prevention of a single major landslide in a community may more than compensate for the effort and cost of implementing a control program (Fleming and Taylor, 1980, p. 20).

Avoiding the costs of litigation is an additional incentive to undertaking a local program of landslide hazard mitigation.

When landslide disasters do occur, the existence of a program for loss reduction should help ensure that redevelopment planning takes existing geologic hazards into account.

In the U.S., only a few communities have established successful landslide loss reduction programs. The most notable is Los Angeles, where, as mentioned above, loss reductions of 97 percent have been achieved for new construction since the implementation of modern grading regulations (Slosson and Krohn, 1982).

In communities that have achieved loss reductions, decisions about building codes, zoning, and land use take into account identified landslide hazards. The U.S. Geological Survey (1982) has found that these communities have in common four preconditions leading to successful mitigation programs: (1) an adequate base of technical information about the local landslide problem, (2) an "able and concerned" local government, (3) a technical community able to apply and add to the technical planning base, and (4) an informed population that supports mitigation program objectives. While the technical expertise to reduce landslide losses is currently available in most states, in many cases it is not being utilized. Still, the success of loss reduction measures clearly depends upon the will of leaders to promote and support mitigation initiatives.

Local Government Roles

At the local government level, hazard mitigation is often a controversial issue. Staff and elected officials of local governments are usually subjected to diverse and sometimes conflicting pressures regarding land use and development. Local officials, as well as builders, realtors, and other parties in the development process, are increasingly being held liable

for actions, or failures to act, that are determined to contribute to personal injuries and property damages caused by natural hazards. Consequently, a model community landslide hazard management planning process should encourage citizen participation and review in order to identify and address the perspectives and concerns of the various community groups affected by landslide hazards.

Because most landslide damages are related to human activity—mainly the construction of roads, utilities, homes, and businesses—the best opportunities for reducing landslide hazards are found in land-use planning and the administration and enforcement of codes and ordinances.

The vulnerability of people to natural hazards is determined by the relationship between the occurrences of extreme events, the proximity of people to these occurrences, and the degree to which the people are prepared to cope with these extremes of nature. The concept of a hazard as the intersection of the human system and the physical system, is illustrated in Figure 5. Only when these two systems are in conflict, does a landslide represent a hazard to public health and safety.

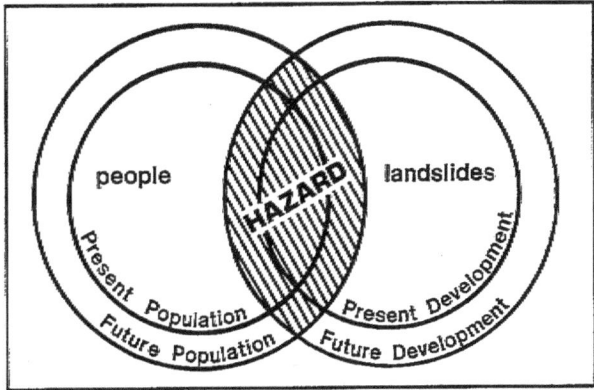

Figure 5. The relationship of people, landslides, and hazards (modified from Colorado Water Conservation Board et al., 1985).

The effectiveness of local landslide mitigation programs is generally tied to the ability and determination of local officials to apply the mitigation techniques available to them to limit and guide growth in hazardous areas. A list of 27 techniques that planners and managers may use to reduce landslide hazards in their communities is presented in Table 2. The key to achieving loss reduction is the identification and implementation of specific mitigation initiatives, as agreed upon and set forth in a local or state landslide hazard mitigation plan.

Table 2. Techniques for reducing landslide hazards (Kockelman, 1986).

Discouraging new developments in hazardous areas by:
- Disclosing the hazard to real-estate buyers
- Posting warnings of potential hazards
- Adopting utility and public-facility service-area policies
- Informing and educating the public
- Making a public record of hazards

Removing or converting existing development through:
- Acquiring or exchanging hazardous properties
- Discontinuing nonconforming uses
- Reconstructing damaged areas after landslides
- Removing unsafe structures
- Clearing and redeveloping blighted areas before landslides

Providing financial incentives or disincentives by:
- Conditioning federal and state financial assistance
- Clarifying the legal liability of property owners
- Adopting lending policies that reflect risk of loss
- Requiring insurance related to level of hazard
- Providing tax credits or lower assessments to property owners

Regulating new development in hazardous areas by:
- Enacting grading ordinances
- Adopting hillside-development regulations
- Amending land-use zoning districts and regulations
- Enacting sanitary ordinances
- Creating special hazard-reduction zones and regulations
- Enacting subdivision ordinances
- Placing moratoriums on rebuilding

Protecting existing development by:
- Controlling landslides and slumps
- Controlling mudflows and debris-flows
- Controlling rockfalls
- Creating improvement districts that assess costs to beneficiaries
- Operating monitoring, warning, and evacuating systems

Although certain opportunities for reducing landslide losses exist at the state government level (selection of sites for schools, hospitals, prisons, and other public facilities; public works projects that protect highways and state property), the greatest potential for mitigation is in the routine operations of local government: the adoption and enforcement of grading and construction codes and ordinances, the development of land-use and open-space plans, elimination of nonconforming uses, limitation of the extension of public utilities, etc. For this reason, state mitigation plans should emphasize mitigation activities that will essentially encourage and support local efforts. Local mitigation plans should provide guidelines and schedules for accomplishing local mitigation projects, as well as identify projects beyond local capability that should be considered in the state plan. ❏

Chapter 3

Causes and Types of Landslides

What is a Landslide?

The term "landslide" is used to describe a wide variety of processes that result in the perceptible downward and outward movement of soil, rock, and vegetation under gravitational influence. The materials may move by: falling, toppling, sliding, spreading, or flowing.

Although landslides are primarily associated with steep slopes, they also can occur in areas of generally low relief. In these areas landslides occur as cut-and-fill failures (highway and building excavations), river bluff failures, lateral spreading landslides, the collapse of mine-waste piles (especially coal), and a wide variety of slope failures associated with quarries and open-pit mines. Underwater landslides on the floors of lakes or reservoirs, or in offshore marine settings, also usually involve areas of low relief and small slope gradients.

Why Do Landslides Occur?

Landslides can be triggered by both natural and man-induced changes in the environment. The geologic history of an area, as well as activities associated with human occupation, directly determines, or contributes to the conditions that lead to slope failure. The basic causes of slope instability are fairly well known. They can be **inherent**, such as weaknesses in the composition or structure of the rock or soil; **variable**, such as heavy rain, snowmelt, and changes in ground-water level; **transient**, such as seismic or volcanic activity; or **due to new environmental conditions**, such as those imposed by construction activity (Varnes and the International Association of Engineering Geology, 1984).

Human Activities

Human activities triggering landslides are mainly associated with construction and involve changes in slope and in surface-water and ground-water regimes. Changes in slope result from terracing for agriculture, cut-and-fill construction for highways, the construction of buildings and railroads, and mining operations. If these activities and facilities are ill-conceived, or improperly designed or constructed, they can increase slope angle, decrease toe or lateral support, or load the head of an existing or potential landslide. Changes in irrigation or surface runoff can cause changes in surface drainage and can increase erosion or contribute to loading a slope or raising the ground-water table (Figure 6). The ground-water table can also be raised by lawn watering, waste-water effluent from leach fields or cesspools, leaking water pipes, swimming pools or ponds, and application or conveyance of irrigation water. A high ground-water level results in increased pore-water pressure and decreased shear strength, thus facilitating slope failure. Conversely, the lowering of the ground-water table as a result of rapid drawdown by water supply wells, or the lowering of a lake or reservoir, can also cause slope failure as the buoyancy provided by the water decreases and seepage gradients steepen.

Natural Factors

There are a number of natural factors that can cause slope failure. Some of these, such as long-term or cyclic climate changes, are not discernible without instrumentation and/or long-term record-keeping.

Climate

Long-term climate changes can have a significant impact on slope stability. An overall decrease in precipitation results in a lowering of the water table, as well as a decrease in the weight of the soil mass, decreased solution of materials, and less intense freeze-thaw activity. An increase in precipitation or ground saturation will raise the level of the ground-water

*Figure 6.
Aerial view of the
Savage Island land-
slide on the east
shore of the
Columbia River,
Washington, 1981.
This landslide was
caused by irrigation
water (photograph
by Robert L.
Schuster, U.S.
Geological Survey).*

table, reduce shear strength, increase the weight of the soil mass, and may increase erosion and freeze-thaw activity. Periodic high-intensity precipitation and rapid snow-melt can signifcantly increase slope instability temporarily (Figure 7).

Erosion

Erosion by intermittent running water (gully ing), streams, rivers, waves or currents, wind, and ice removes toe and lateral slope support of potential landslides.

Weathering

Weathering is the natural process of rock deter-ioration which produces weak, landslide-prone materials. It is caused by the chemical action of air, water, plants, and bacteria and the physical

*Figure 7.
The remains of a
house where three
children died in a
mudflow in Kanawha
City, West Virginia.
The movement was
triggered by heavy
rainfall from a cloud-
burst on July 9, 1973
(Lessing et al., 1976).*

action brought on by changes in temperature (expansion and shrinkage), the freeze-thaw cycle, and the burrowing activity of animals.

Earthquakes

Earthquakes not only trigger landslides, but, over time, the tectonic activity causing them can create steep and potentially unstable slopes.

Rapid sedimentation

Rivers supply very large amounts of sediment to deltas in lakes and coastal areas. The rapidly deposited sediments are frequently under-consolidated, and have excess pore-water pressures and low strengths. Such deltaic sediments are often prone to underwater delta-front landsliding, especially where the sediments are rich in clay and/or contain gas from organic decomposition.

Wind-generated waves

Storm waves in coastal areas are known to trigger underwater landsliding in deltas by cyclically loading weak bottom sediments.

Tidal or river drawdown

Rapid lowering of water level in coastal areas or along river banks due to tides or river discharge fluctuations can cause underwater landsliding. The process in which weak river bank or deltaic sediments are left unsupported as the water level drops is known as "drawdown."

Types of Landslides

The most common types of landslides are described below. These definitions are based mainly on the work of Varnes (1978).

Falls

Falls are abrupt movements of masses of geologic materials that become detached from steep slopes or cliffs (Figures 8a, b). Movement occurs by free-fall, bouncing, and rolling. Depending on the type of earth materials involved, the result is a rockfall, soilfall, debris fall, earth fall, boulder fall, and so on. All types of falls are promoted by undercutting, differential weathering, excavation, or stream erosion.

Topple

A topple is a block of rock that tilts or rotates forward on a pivot or hinge point and then

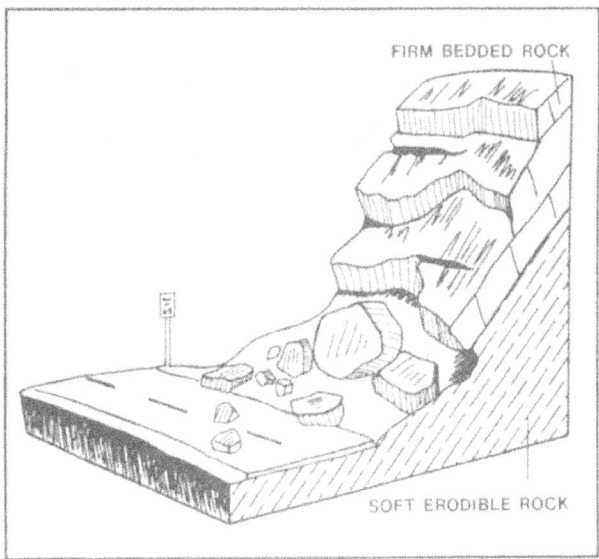

Figure 8a. Rockfall (Colorado Geological Survey et al., 1988).

Figure 8b. Rockfall on U.S. Highway 6, Colorado (photograph by Colorado Geological Survey).

separates from the main mass, falling to the slope below, and subsequently bouncing or rolling down the slope (Figures 9a, b).

Slides

Although many types of mass movement are included in the general term "landslide," the more restrictive use of the term refers to movements of soil or rock along a distinct surface of rupture which separates the slide material from more stable underlying material. The two major types of landslides are rotational slides and translational slides.

11

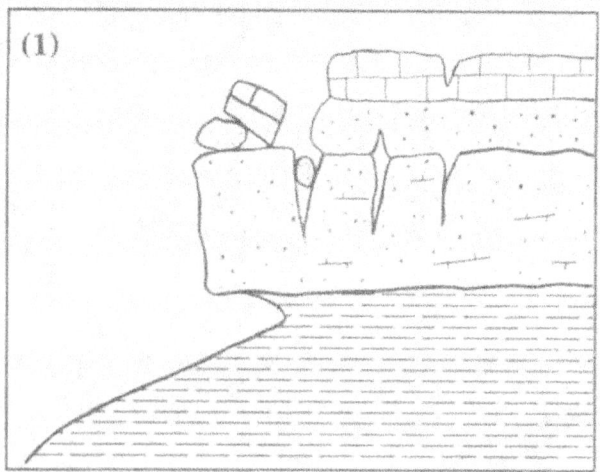

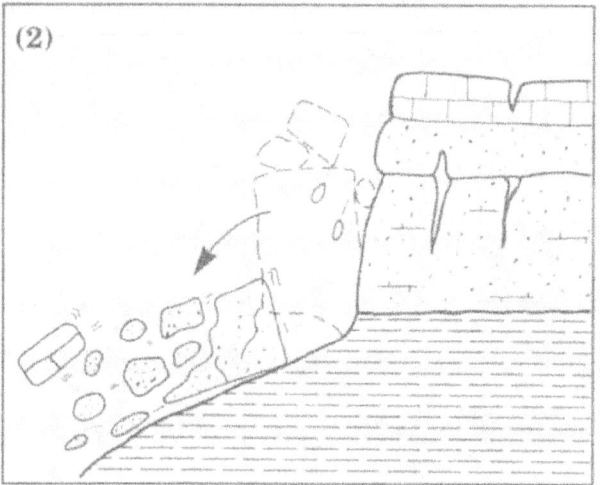

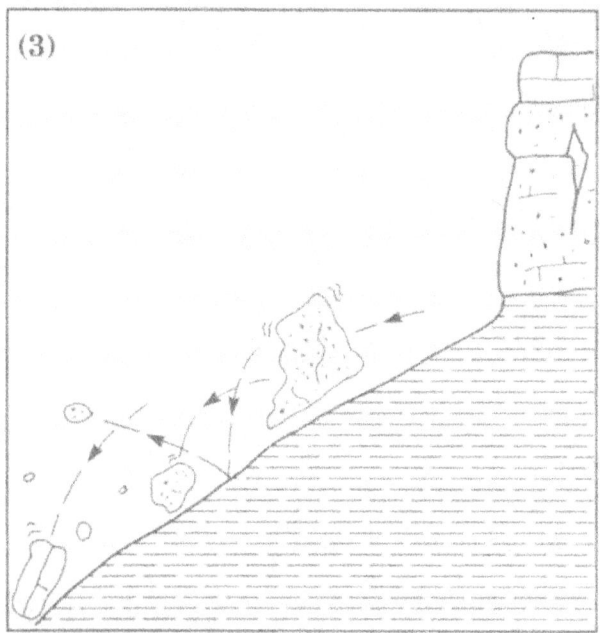

Figure 9a. Topple (Colorado Geological Survey et al., 1988).

Figure 9b. Topple, western Colorado (photograph by Colorado Geological Survey).

Rotational slide

A rotational slide is one in which the surface of rupture is curved concavely upward (spoon shaped) and the slide movement is more or less rotational about an axis that is parallel to the contour of the slope (Figures 10a, b). A "slump" is an example of a small rotational slide.

Translational slide

In a translational slide, the mass moves out, or down and outward along a relatively planar surface and has little rotational movement or backward tilting (Figure 11). The mass commonly slides out on top of the original ground surface. Such a slide may progress over great

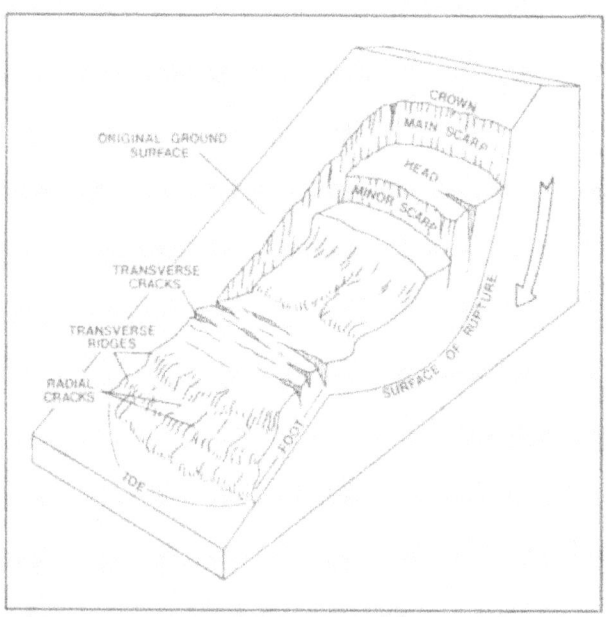

Figure 10a. Rotational landslide (modified from Varnes, 1978).

Figure 10b. Rotational landslide, Golden, Colorado (photograph by Colorado Geological Survey).

distances if conditions are right. Slide material may range from loose unconsolidated soils to extensive slabs of rock.

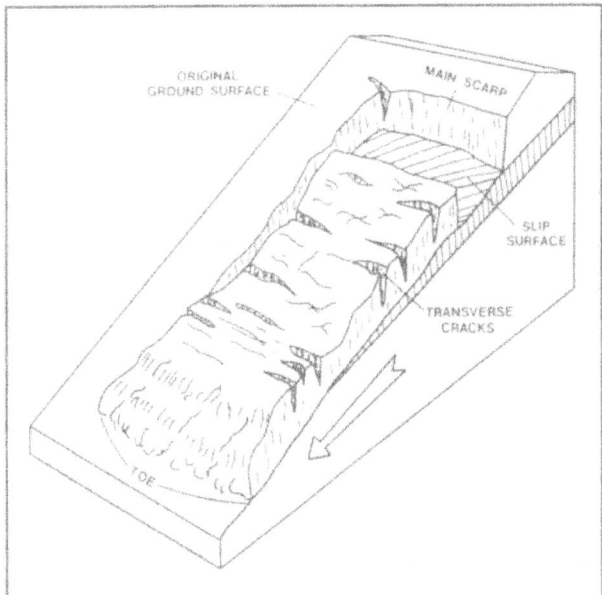

Figure 11. Translational slide (Colorado Geological Survey et al., 1988).

Block Slide. A block slide is a translational slide in which the moving mass consists of a single unit, or a few closely related units that move downslope as a single unit (Figure 12).

Lateral Spreads

Lateral spreads (Figures 13a, b) are a result of the nearly horizontal movement of geologic

materials and are distinctive because they usually occur on very gentle slopes. The failure is caused by liquefaction, the process whereby saturated, loose, cohesionless sediments (usually sands and silts) are transformed from a solid into a liquefied state; or plastic flow of subjacent material. Failure is usually triggered by rapid ground motion such as that experienced during an earthquake, or by slow chemcal changes in the pore water and mineral constituents.

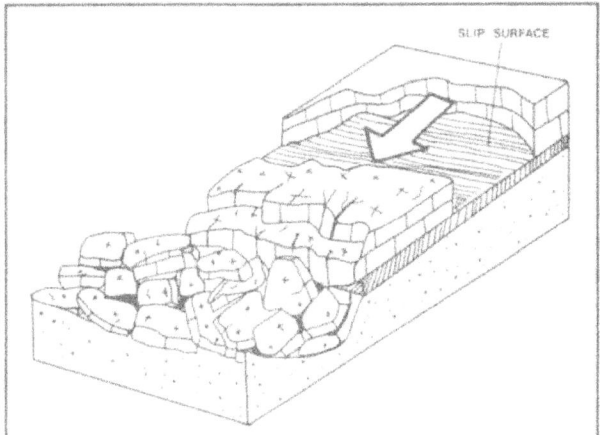

Figure 12 . Block slide (Colorado Geological Survey et al., 1988).

Flows

Creep
Creep is the imperceptibly slow, steady downward movement of slope-forming soil or rock. Creep is indicated by curved tree trunks, bent fences or retaining walls, tilted poles or fences, and small soil ripples or terracettes (Figures 14a, b).

Debris flow
A debris flow is a form of rapid mass movement in which loose soils, rocks, and organic matter combine with entrained air and water to form a slurry that then flows downslope. Debris-flow areas are usually associated with steep gullies. Individual debris-flow areas can usually be identified by the presence of debris fans at the termini of the drainage basins (Figure 15).

Debris avalanche
A debris avalanche is a variety of very rapid to extremely rapid debris flow.

Earthflow

Earthflows have a characteristic "hourglass" shape (Figures 16a, b). A bowl or depression forms at the head where the unstable material collects and flows out. The central area is narrow and usually becomes wider as it reaches the valley floor. Flows generally occur in fine-grained materials or clay-bearing rocks on moderate slopes and with saturated conditions. However, dry flows of granular material are also possible.

Mudflow

A mudflow is an earthflow that consists of material that is wet enough to flow rapidly and that contains at least 50 percent sand-, silt-, and clay-sized particles.

Lahar

A lahar is a mudflow or debris flow that originates on the slope of a volcano. Lahars are usually triggered by such things as heavy rainfall eroding volcanic deposits; sudden melting of snow and ice due to heat from volcanic vents; or by the breakout of water from glaciers, crater lakes, or lakes dammed by volcanic eruptions.

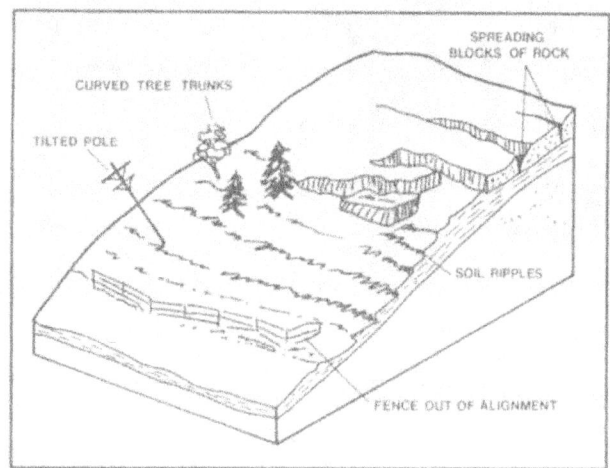

Figure 14a. Creep (Colorado Geological Survey et al., 1988).

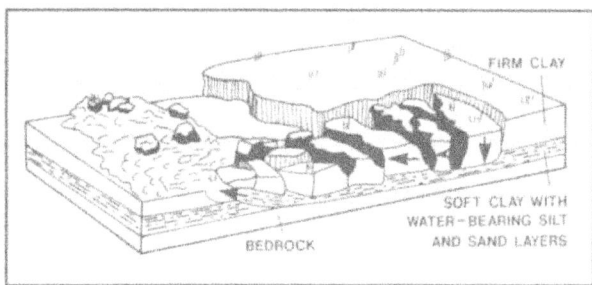

Figure 13a. Lateral spread (Colorado Geological Survey et al., 1988).

Figure 13b. Lateral spread, Cortez, Colorado. (Photograph by Colorado Geological Survey).

Figure 14b. Creep, vicinity of Mt. Vernon Canyon, Jefferson County, Colorado (photograph by Colorado Geological Survey).

14

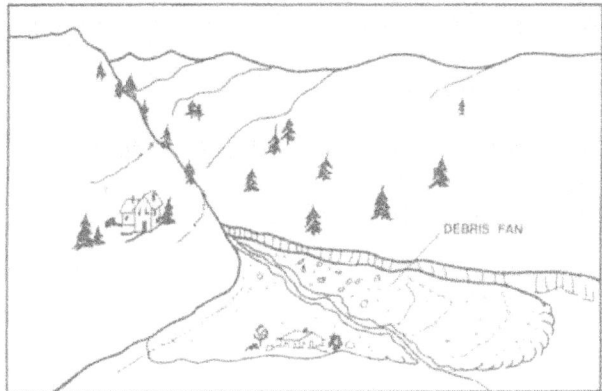

Figure 15. Debris fan formed by debris flows (Colorado Geological Survey et al., 1988).

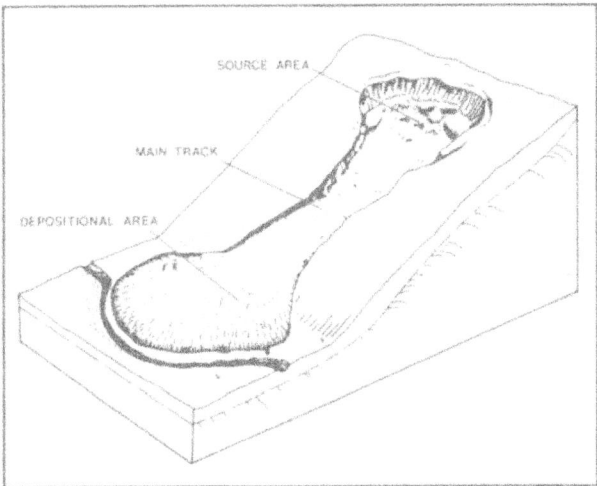

Figure 16a. Earthflow (modified from Varnes, 1978).

Figure 16b. Roan Creek earthflow near DeBeque, Colorado, 1985 (photograph by Colorado Geological Survey).

Subaqueous landslide *

Landslides which take place principally or totally underwater in lakes, along river banks, or in coastal and offshore marine areas are called subaqueous landslides. The failure of subaqueous slopes may result from a variety of factors acting singly or together, including rapid lacustrine or marine sedimentation, biogenic methane gas in sediments, surface water storm waves, current scour, water level drawdown, depositional oversteeping, or earthquake stresses. Many different types of subaqueous landslides have been identified in different locations, including rotational and translational slides, debris flows and mudflows, sand and silt liquefaction flows. There is also evidence that, in some circumstances, subaqueous landslides evolve into or initiate turbidity currents, which may flow underwater at high speeds for long distances. Subaqueous landslides pose problems for offshore and river engineering, particularly for the construction and maintenance of jetties, piers, levees, offshore platforms and facilities, and for sea-bed installations such as pipelines and telecommunications cables.

Interrelationship of Landsliding with Other Natural Hazards (The Multiple Hazard Concept)

Natural hazards often occur simultaneously or, in some cases, one hazard triggers another. For example, an earthquake may trigger a landslide, which in turn may block a valley causing upstream flooding. Different hazards may also occur at the same time as the result of a common cause. For example, heavy precipitation or rapid snowmelt can cause debris flows and flooding in the same area.

The simultaneous or sequential occurrence of interactive hazards may produce cumulative effects that differ significantly from those expected from any one of the component hazards.

Landsliding and Dam Safety

The safety of a dam can be severely compromised by landsliding upstream from the dam or on slopes bordering the dam's reservoir or abutments. Possible impacts include (1) the forma-

*Discussion by D.B. Prior

tion of wave surges that can overtop the dam, (2) increased sedimentation with resulting loss of storage, and (3) dam failure.

Flood surges can be generated either by the sudden detachment of large masses of earth into the reservoir, or by the formation and subsequent failure of a landslide dam across an upstream tributary stream channel. Waves formed by such failures can overtop the dam and cause serious downstream flooding without actually causing structural failure of the dam.

Landsliding into upstream areas or reservoirs can greatly increase the amount of sediment that is deposited in the reservoir, ultimately reducing storage capacity. This increases the likelihood that the dam will be overtopped during periods of excessive runoff, causing downstream flooding. Excessive sedimentation can also damage pumps and intake valves associated with water systems and hydroelectric plants.

Actual dam failure could be caused by landsliding at or near the abutments or in the embankments of earthen dams.

In 1983 a large mass of rock detached from Slide Mountain in Nevada. The mass slid into Upper Price Lake, an irrigation reservoir, displacing most of the water which overtopped and breached the dam, flowing into Lower Price Lake. This lake's dam was also breached. The water flowed into Ophir Creek where it collected large amounts of debris and became a debris

flow. After traveling about four kilometers and dropping 600 meters in elevation, the debris flow emerged from the canyon onto the alluvial fan of Ophir Creek (total time—15 minutes). One person was killed, four injured, and numerous houses and vehicles were destroyed (Figure 17) (Watters, 1988).

Rapid changes in the water level of reservoirs can also trigger landslides. When the water level in the reservoir is lowered (rapid drawdown), the subsequent loss of support provided by the water and increased seepage pressure can initiate sliding (Figure 18). Alternatively, the increase in saturation caused by rising water can trigger landslides on slopes bordering the reservoir.

Eisbacher and Clague (1984) describe an excellent example of the potential impacts of landsliding on dam safety: the 1963 Vaiont dam disaster in Italy. The Vaiont Dam, a hydroelectric dam, was completed in 1960 to impound the Vaiont Torrent, a major tributary of the Piave River in the southern Alps of Italy. The dam is 261 m high and spans a steep narrow gorge. The southern wall of the valley behind the dam is a steep dip slope. Within two months after the reservoir was filled, a 0.7×10^6 m^3 mass of rock slumped away along the submerged toe of the southern embankment. Over time, deep-seated movement of the slope occurred in response to changing levels of the reservoir. As a result of these movements,

Figure 17. House destroyed by 1983 Slide Mountain, Nevada landslide (photograph by Robert J. Watters, University of Nevada, Reno).

Figure 18. Jackson Springs landslide on the Spokane arm of Franklin D. Roosevelt Lake, Washington, 1969. This landslide was triggered by extreme drawdown of the lake (photograph by the U.S. Bureau of Reclamation).

monitoring instruments were set up on the slope.In August and September of 1963, precipitation in the Piave Valley was three times higher than normal and infiltration of the precipitation into the slope probably contributed to its eventual failure. The day before the catastrophic slope failure creep rates of 40cm/day were registered.

On October 9–10, 1963, in the night, a large slab of the unstable slope failed and slipped into the reservoir. The volume of material was estimated to be 250×10^6 m^3 (a slab 250 m thick). A wall of water 250 m high surged up the opposite side of the valley, then turned and overtopped the dam. The concrete dam held, and the wall of water (30×10^6 m^3) dropped into the narrow gorge below, scouring loose debris as it went and destroying several communities below the dam. At least 1,900 people were killed.

The site of the dam has been left as it remained after the disaster, as a monument.

Landsliding and Flooding

Landsliding and flooding are closely allied because both are related to precipitation, run-off, and ground saturation. In addition, debris flows usually occur in small, steep stream channels and often are mistaken for floods. In fact, these events frequently occur simultaneously in the same area, and there is no distinct line differentiating the two phenomena.

Landslides and debris flows can cause flooding by forming landslide dams that block valleys and stream channels, allowing large amounts of water to back-up (Figure 19). This causes backwater flooding and, if the dam breaks, subsequent downstream flooding. Also, soil and debris from landslides can "bulk" or add volume to otherwise normal stream flow or cause channel blockages and diversions creating flood conditions or localized erosion. Finally, large landslides can negate the protective functions of a dam by reducing reservoir capacity or creating surge waves that can overtop a

17

dam, resulting in downstream flooding (as described above).

In turn, flooding can cause landsliding. Erosion, due to rapidly moving flood waters, often undercuts slopes or cliffs. Once support is removed from the base of saturated slopes, landsliding often ensues.

Landsliding and Seismic Activity

Most of the mountainous areas that are vulnerable to landslides have also experienced at least moderate seismicity in historic times. The occurrence of earthquakes in steep landslide-prone areas greatly increases the likelihood that landslides will occur and increases the risk of serious damage far beyond that posed individually by the two processes.

Landslide materials can be dilated by seismic activity and thus be subject to rapid infiltration during rainfall and snowmelt. Some areas of high seismic potential such as the New Madrid Seismic Zone of the lower Mississippi River valley may be subject to liquefaction and related ground failure. The Great Alaska Earthquake of March 27, 1964 caused an estimated $300 million in damages. As mentioned eariler, 60 percent of this was due to ground failure. Five landslides caused about $50 million damage in the city of Anchorage. Lateral spread failures damaged highways, railroads, and bridges, costing another $50 million. Flow failures in three Alaskan ports carried away docks, warehouses, and adjacent transportation facilities accounting for another $15

Figure 19. Aerial view of the Thistle landslide, Utah, 1983. This landslide dammed the Spanish Fork River creating a lake which inundated the town of Thistle and severed three major transportation arteries (photograph by Robert L. Schuster, U.S. Geological Survey).

million. Much of the landsliding was a direct result of the effect of the severe ground shaking on the Bootlegger Cove Formation. The shaking caused loss of strength in clays and liquefaction in sand and silt lenses (U.S. Geological Survey, 1981a).

Landsliding and Volcanic Activity

The May 18, 1980 eruption of Mount St. Helens in Washington state triggered a massive landslide on the north flank of the mountain. The volume of material moved was estimated to be 2.73 km^3. The landslide effectively depressurized the interior of the volcano; superheated waters turned into steam and magmatic gases also expanded, resulting in a giant explosion (U.S. Geological Survey, 1981b).

Because human activity had been restricted in the Mount St. Helens area due to predictions of an eruption, loss of life was minimized. However, the eruption devastated land as far as 29 km from the volcano. The resulting lateral blast, landslides, debris avalanches, debris flows, and flooding took 57 lives and caused an estimated $860 million in damage (Advisory Committee on the International Decade for Natural Hazard Reduction, 1987). ❑

Chapter 4
Hazard Identification, Assessment, and Mapping

Hazard Analysis

Recognition of the presence of active or potential slope movement, and of the types and causes of the movement, is essential to landslide mitigation. Recognition depends on an accurate evaluation of the geology, hydrogeology, landforms, and interrelated factors such as environmental conditions and human activities. Only trained professionals should conduct such evaluations. However, because local governments may need to contract for such services, they should be aware of the techniques available and their advantages and limitations.

Techniques for recognizing the presence or potential development of landslides include:

- map analysis
- analysis of aerial photography and imagery
- analysis of acoustic imagery and profiles
- field reconnaissance
- aerial reconnaissance
- drilling
- acoustic imaging and profiling
- geophysical studies
- computerized landslide terrain analysis
- instrumentation

Map Analysis

Map analysis is usually one of the first steps in a landslide investigation. Maps that can be used include geologic, topographic, soils, and geomorphic. Using knowledge of geologic materials and processes, a trained person can obtain a general idea of landslide susceptibility from such maps.

Analysis of Aerial Photography and Imagery

The analysis of aerial photography is a quick and valuable technique for identifying landslides, because it provides a three-dimensional overview of the terrain and indicates human activities as well as much geologic information. In addition, the availability of many types of aerial imagery (satellite, infrared, radar, etc.) make this a very versatile technique.

Analysis of Acoustic Imagery and Profiles*

Profiles of lake beds, river bottoms, and the sea floor can be obtained using acoustic techniques such as side-scan sonar and subbottom seismic profiling. Surveying of controlled grids, with accurate navigation, can yield three-dimensional perspectives of subaqueous geologic phenomena. Modern, high resolution techniques are used routinely in offshore shelf areas to map geologic hazards for offshore engineering. Surveying and mapping standards for outer continental shelf regions are regulated by the U.S. Minerals Management Service.

Field Reconnaissance

Many of the more subtle signs of slope movement cannot be identified on maps or photographs. Indeed, if an area is heavily forested or has been urbanized, even major features may not be evident. Furthermore, landslide features change over time on an active slide. Thus, field reconnaissance is necessary to verify or detect many landslide features.

Aerial Reconnaissance

Low-level flights in helicopters or small aircraft can be used to obtain a rapid and direct overview of a site.

Drilling

At most sites, drilling is necessary to determine the type of earth materials involved in the slide, the depth to the slip surface and thus the thickness and geometry of the landslide mass, the water-table level, and the degree of disruption

*By D.B. Prior

20

of the landslide materials. It can also provide samples for age-dating and testing the engineering properties of landslide materials. Finally, drilling is needed for installation of some monitoring instruments and hydrologic observation wells.

Geophysical Studies

Geophysical techniques (the study of changes in the earth's gravitational and electrical fields, or measurement of induced seismic behavior) can be used to determine some subsurface characteristics such as the depth to bedrock, zones of saturation, and sometimes the ground-water table. It can also be used to determine the degree of consolidation of subsurface materials and the geometry of the units involved. In most instances these methods can best be used to supplement drilling information. Monitoring of natural acoustic emissions from moving soil or rock has also been used in landslide studies.

Computerized Landslide Terrain Analysis

In recent years computer modeling of landslides has been used to determine the volume of landslide masses and changes in surface expression and cross section over time. This information is useful in calculating the potential for stream blockage, cost of landslide removal (based on volume), and type and mechanism of movement. Very promising methods are being developed utilizing digital elevation models (DEMs) to evaluate areas quickly for their susceptibility to landslide/debris-flow events (Filson, 1987; Ellen and Mark, 1988). Computers are also being used to perform complex stability analyses. Software programs for these studies are readily available for personal computers.

Instrumentation

Sophisticated methods such as electronic distance measuring (EDM); instruments such as inclinometers, extensometers, strain meters, tiltmeters, and piezometers; and simple techniques such as establishing control points using stakes can all be used to determine the mechanics of landslide movement and to warn against impending slope failure.

Anticipating the Landslide Hazard

One of the guiding principles of geology is that the past is the key to the future. In evaluating landslide hazards this means that future slope failures will probably occur as a result of the same geologic, geomorphic, and hydrologic situations that led to past and present failures. Based on this assumption, it is possible to estimate the types, frequency of occurrence, extent, and consequences of slope failures that may occur in the future. However, the absence of past events in a specific area does not preclude future failures. Man-induced conditions such as changes in the natural topography or hydrologic conditions can create or increase an area's susceptibility to slope failure (Varnes and the International Association of Engineering Geology, 1984).

In order to predict landslide hazards in an area, the conditions and processes that promote instability must be identified and their relative contributions to slope failure estimated, if possible. Useful conclusions concerning **increased probability** of landsliding can be drawn by combining geological analyses with knowledge of short- and long-term meteorological conditions. Current technology enables persons monitoring earth movements to define those areas most susceptible to landsliding and to issue "alerts" covering time spans of hours to days when meteorological conditions known to increase or initiate certain types of landslides occur. Alerts covering longer periods of time become proportionately less reliable.

Translation of Technical Information to Users

According to Kockelman (personal communication, 1989), the successful translation of natural hazard information for nontechnical users conveys the following three elements in one form or another:

(1) likelihood of the occurrence of an event of a size and location that would cause casualties, damage, or disruption;

(2) location and extent of the effects of the event on the ground, structures, or socioeconomic activity;

(3) estimated severity of the effects on the ground, structures, or socioeconomic activity.

These elements are needed because usually engineers, planners, and decision makers will not be concerned with a potential hazard if its likelihood is rare, its location is unknown, or its severity is slight.

Unfortunately, these three pieces of information can come in different forms with many different names, some quantitative and precise, others qualitative and general. For a product to qualify as "translated" hazard information, the nontechnical user must be able to perceive likelihood, location, and severity of the hazard so that he or she becomes aware of the danger, can convey the risk to others, and can use the translated information directly in a reduction technique.

Maps are a useful and convenient tool for presenting information on landslide hazards. They can present many kinds and combinations of information at different levels of detail. Hazard maps used in conjunction with land-use maps are a valuable planning tool. Leighton (1976) suggests a three-stage approach to landslide hazard mapping. The first stage is regional or reconnaissance mapping, which synthesizes available data and identifies general problem areas. This small-scale mapping is usually performed by a state or federal geological survey. The next stage is community-level mapping, a more detailed surface and subsurface mapping program in complex problem areas. Finally, detailed site-specific large-scale maps are prepared. If resources are limited, it may be more prudent to bypass regional mapping and concentrate on a few known areas of concern.

Regional Mapping

Regional or reconnaissance mapping supplies basic data for regional planning, for conducting more detailed studies at the community and site-specific levels, and for setting priorities for future mapping.

These maps are usually simple inventory maps and are directed primarily toward the identification and delineation of regional landslide problem areas and the conditions under which they occur. They concentrate on those

geologic units or environments in which additional movements are most likely. Such mapping relies heavily on photogeology (the geologic interpretation of aerial photography), reconnaissance field mapping, and the collection and synthesis of all available pertinent geologic data (Leighton, 1976).

Regional maps are most often prepared at a scale of 1:24,000, because high-quality U.S. Geological Survey topographic base maps at this scale are widely available, and aerial photos are commonly of a comparable scale. Other scales commonly used include 1:50,000 (county series), 1:100,000 (30 x 60 minute series), and 1:250,000 (1 x 2 degree series).

Community-Level Mapping

Community-level mapping identifies both the three-dimensional limits of landslides and their causes. Guidance concerning land use, zoning, and building, as well as recommendations for future site-specific investigations, are also made at this stage. Investigations should include subsurface exploratory work in order to produce a large-scale map with cross sections (Leighton, 1976). Map scales at this level vary from 1:1,000 to 1:10,000.

Site-Specific Mapping

Site-specific mapping is concerned with the identification, analysis, and solution of actual site-specific problems. It is usually undertaken by private consultants for landowners who propose site development and typically involves a detailed drilling program with downhole logging, sampling, and laboratory analysis in order to procure the necessary information for design and construction (Leighton, 1976). Map scales vary, but are usually not larger than one inch equal to 50 feet.

Types of Maps

The three types of landslide maps most useful to planners and the general public are (1) landslide inventories, (2) landslide susceptibility maps, and (3) landslide hazard maps.

Landslide inventories

Inventories identify areas that appear to have failed by landslide processes, including debris flows and cut-and-fill failures. The level of detail of these maps ranges from simple reconnaissance inventories that only delineate broad areas where landsliding appears to have occurred (Figure 20) to complex inventories that depict and classify each landslide and show scarps, zones of depletion and accumulation, active versus inactive slides, geological age, rate of movement, and other pertinent data on depth and kind of materials involved in sliding (U.S. Geological Survey, 1982; Brabb, 1984b) (Figure 21).

Simple inventories give an overview of the landslide hazard in an area and delineate areas where more detailed studies should be conducted. Detailed inventories provide a better understanding of the different landslide processes operating in an area and can be used to regulate or prevent development in landslide areas and to aid the design of remedial measures (U.S. Geological Survey, 1982). They also provide a good basis for the preparation of derivative maps such as those indicating slope stability, landslide hazard, and land use. Wieczorek (1984) described how to prepare a landslide inventory map that can be used by planners and decision makers to assess landslide hazards on a regional or community level. The process consists of using aerial photography with selective field checking to detect landslide areas, and then presenting the information in map form using a coded format. The maps show any or all of the following: state of activity, certainty of identification, dominant types of slope movement, estimated thickness of slide material, and dates or periods of activity.

Landslide susceptibility maps

A landslide susceptibility map goes beyond an inventory map and depicts areas that have the potential for landsliding (Figure 22). These areas are determined by correlating some of the principal factors that contribute to landsliding, such as steep slopes, weak geologic units that lose strength when saturated, and poorly drained rock or soil, with the past distribution of landslides. These maps indicate only the relative stability of slopes; they do not make absolute predictions (Brabb, 1984b).

Landslide susceptibility maps can be considered derivatives of landslide inventory maps because an inventory is essential for preparing a susceptibility map. Overlaying a geologic map with an inventory map that shows existing landslides can identify specific landslide-prone geologic units. This information can then be extrapolated to predict other areas of

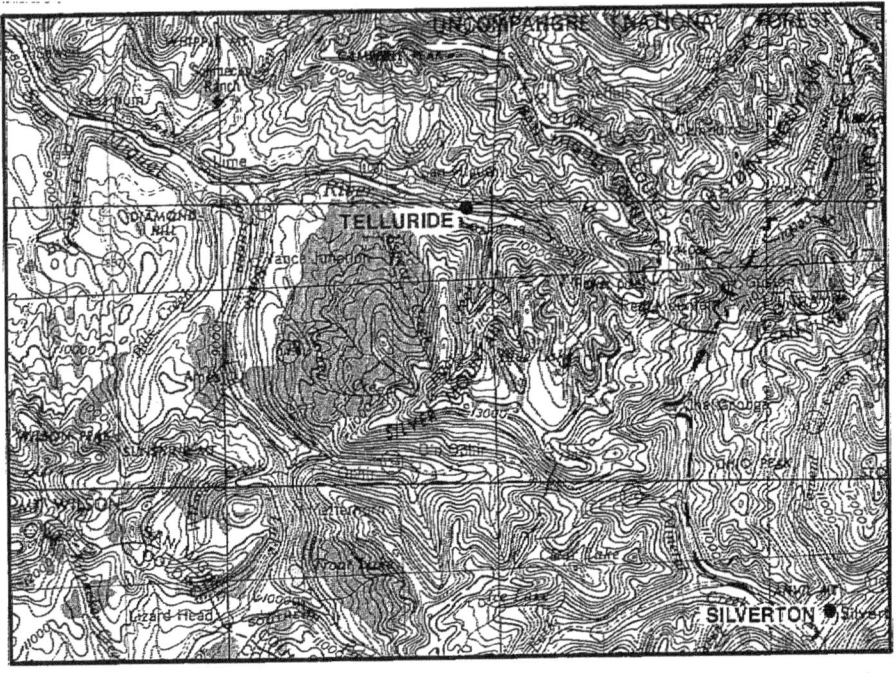

EXPLANATION

Areas inferred to be underlain by landslide deposits

N

Scale 1:250,000

Figure 20. Detail from the landslide inventory map of the Durango 1 x 2 degree map, Colorado (Colton et al., 1975).

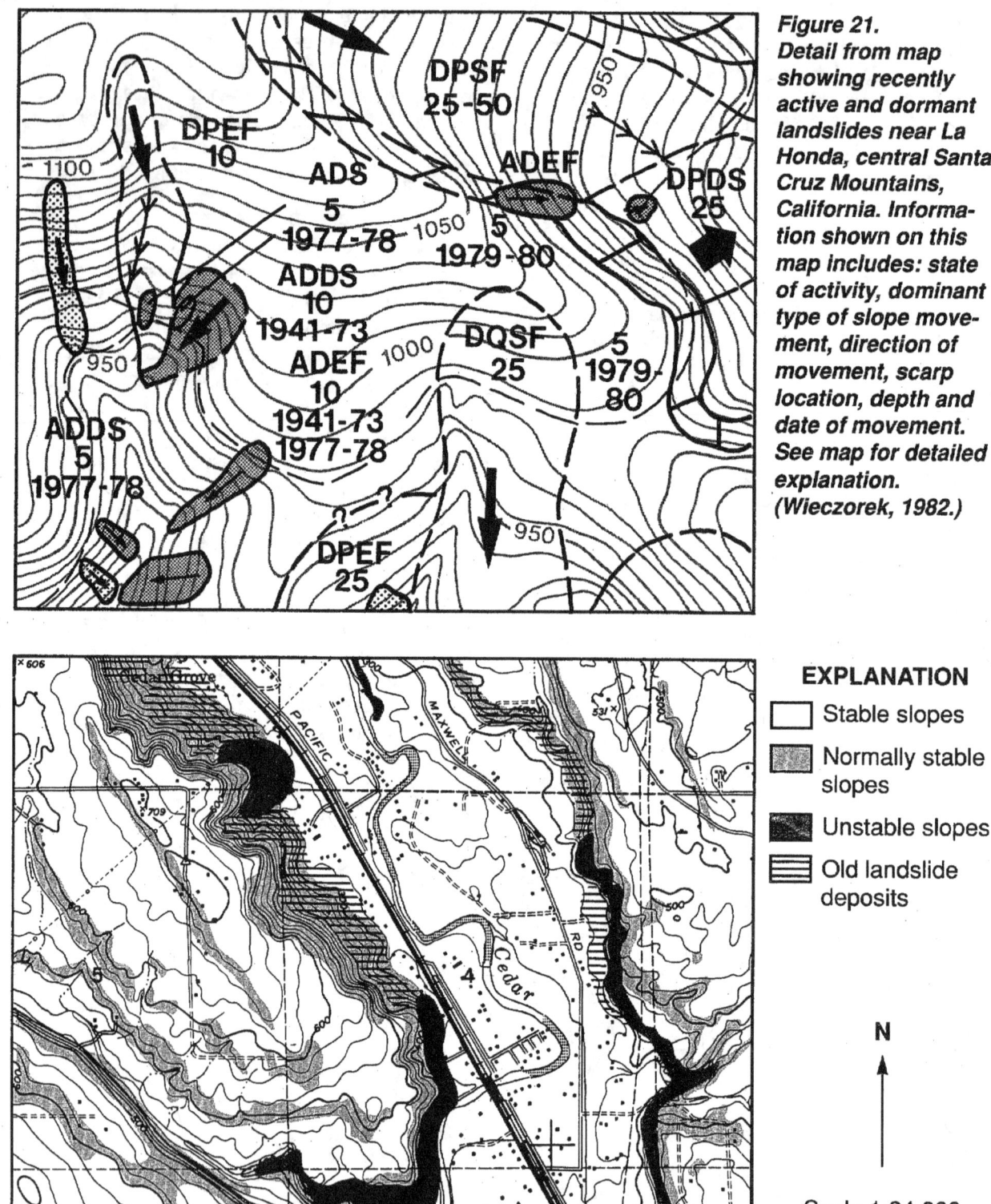

Figure 21.
Detail from map showing recently active and dormant landslides near La Honda, central Santa Cruz Mountains, California. Information shown on this map includes: state of activity, dominant type of slope movement, direction of movement, scarp location, depth and date of movement. See map for detailed explanation. (Wieczorek, 1982.)

EXPLANATION

☐ Stable slopes

▨ Normally stable slopes

▦ Unstable slopes

☰ Old landslide deposits

N

Scale 1:24,000

Figure 22. Detail from map showing relative slope stability in part of west-central King County, Washington (Miller, 1973).

potential landsliding. More complex maps may include additional information such as slope, angle, and drainage.

Landslide hazard maps

Hazard maps show the areal extent of threatening processes: where landslide processes have occurred in the past, where they occur now, and the likelihood in various areas that a landslide will occur in the future (Figure 23). For a given area, they contain detailed information on the types of landslides, extent of slope subject to failure, and probable maximum extent of ground movement. These maps can be used to predict the relative degree of hazard in a landslide area.

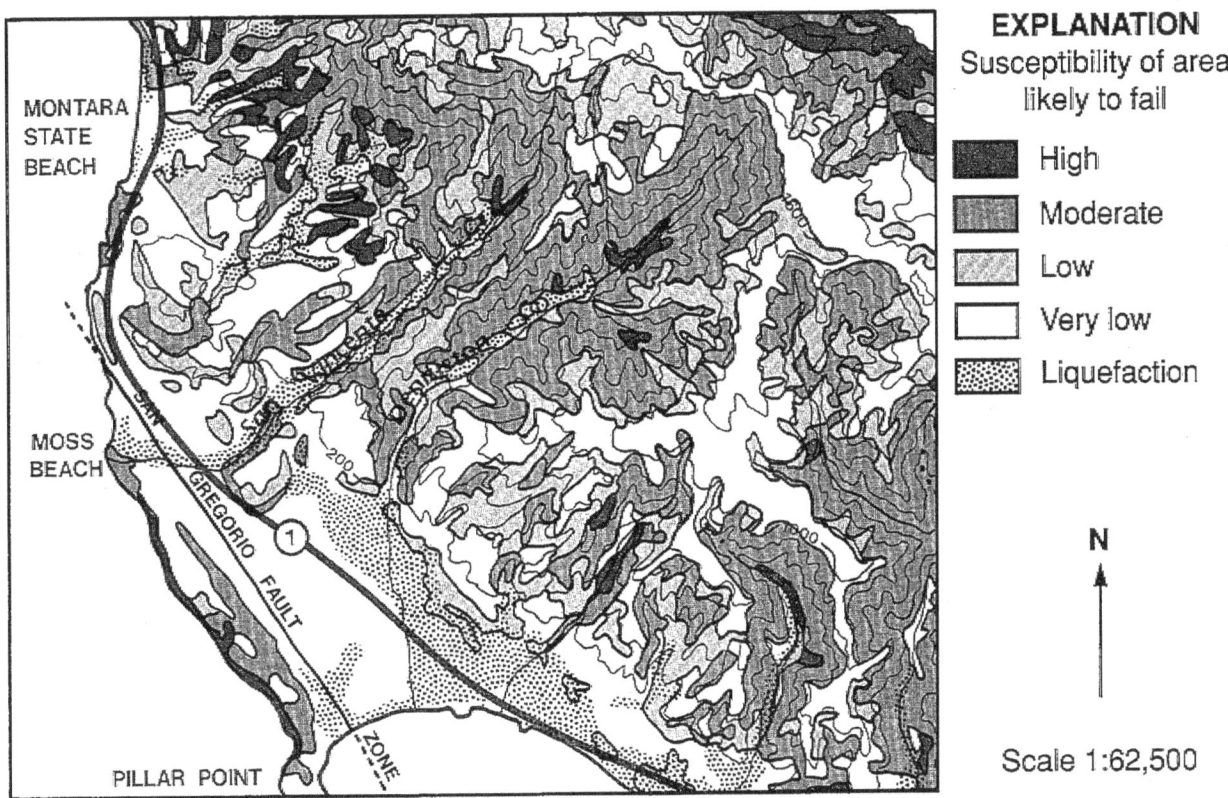

Figure 23. Detail from map showing slope stability during earthquakes in San Mateo County, California (Wieczorek et al., 1985).

Chapter 5
Transferring and Encouraging the Use of Information

A major part of any effective landslide loss-reduction program must be the communication and use of technical information (information transfer). Often individuals or groups do not take mitigative action because they do not understand what to do, or lack training on how to do it. The mitigation and/or avoidance of landslide hazards and the reduction of landslide losses require that appropriate information be communicated to, and effectively used by, planners, decision makers, and emergency response personnel.

According to Kockelman (personal communication, 1989), various terms are used to describe the transfer of information to users, namely "disseminate," "communicate," "circulate," "promulgate," and "distribute." Often these terms are interpreted conservatively. For example, an agency or person might simply issue a press release on hazards or distribute research information to potential users. Such activity rarely results in the adoption of effective hazard reduction techniques.

Kockelman notes that no clear, concise definition or criteria for effective information transfer has been offered or can be found in the literature, except by inference or by analysis of what actually works for lay persons. Therefore, he uses "transfer" to mean the delivery of an understandable product in a usable format to a specific person or group "interested" in, or responsible for, hazard reduction, plus assistance and encouragement in the selection and adoption of an appropriate reduction technique. Only when all these criteria have been met have researchers, translators, and transfer agents fulfilled their objectives.

The effective use of landslide information to reduce danger, damages, or other losses depends not only on the efforts of the producers of the information, but also on (1) the users' interest, capabilities, and experience in hazard-related activities, (2) the existence of enabling legislation authorizing federal, state, and local hazard-reduction activities, (3) the availability of funds and adequate, sufficiently detailed information in a readily usable and understandable form, (4) the use of effective information communication techniques, and (5) the existence of qualified staff at all levels of government with the authority to take mitigative action.

Information Transfer

Methods for transferring and/or obtaining landslide information are listed in Table 3. These methods should be used by any landslide information collection, interpretation, and transferral program designed for planners and decision makers. Some of these services are provided by state agencies, map sales offices, geologic inquiries staffs, public inquiries offices, universities, and, in the course of ordinary day-to-day contacts with the public, by the producers of landslide hazard information. In addition, many research workers have provided such services on a limited and informal basis.

Table 3. Examples of resources available for obtaining / transferring landslide information (adapted from U.S. Geological Survey, 1982).

Educational Services

- Universities and their extension divisions through courses, lectures, books, and display materials
- Guest speakers and participants at lectures in regional and community educational programs related to the application of hazard information
- Seminars, conferences, workshops, short courses, technology utilization sessions, training symposia, and other discussions involving user groups

Table 3. Continued

- Oral briefings, newsletters, seminars, map-type "interpretive inventories," open-file reports, reports of cooperating agencies, and "official-use only" materials (released via news media)
- Radio and television programs that explain or report hazard-reduction programs and products
- Meetings with local, district, and state agencies and their governing bodies
- Field trips to potentially hazardous sites by state, local, or federal agencies, and professional societies

Information Sources

- Annotated and indexed bibliographies of hazard information and lists of pertinent reference materials
- Local, state, and federal policies, procedures, ordinances, statutes, and regulations that cite or make other use of hazards information
- Hazards information incorporated into local, state, and federal studies and plans
- User guides relating to earth-hazards processes, mapping, and hazard-reduction techniques

Users of Landslide Hazard Information

Among the potential users of landslide hazard information are people at national, state, regional, and community levels in both the public and private sectors. Three general categories can be identified: (1) scientists and engineers who use the information directly, (2) planners and decision makers who consider hazards among other land-use and development criteria, (3) developers and builders; financial and insuring organizations, and (4) interested citizens, educators, and others with little or no technical expertise. These people differ widely in the kinds of information they need **and in their capabilities to use that information**. Examples of potential users are listed in Table 4.

Table 4. Potential users of landslide hazard information (modified from U.S. Geological Survey, 1982).

City, County, and Area-Wide Government Users

City and county building, engineering, zoning, safety, planning, and environmental health departments
City and county offices of emergency services
County tax assessors
Local government geologists
Mayors, county commissioners, and city council members
Multicounty (regional) planning, development, and emergency preparedness agencies
Municipal engineers, planners, and administrators
Police, fire, and sheriff's departments
Public works departments
Road departments
School districts
Special districts (water, sanitation, urban drainage)

State Government Users*

Attorney General's Office
Department of Administration
     State Buildings Division
Department of Health
Department of Highways
Department of Local Affairs
Department of Military Affairs
     National Guard
Department of Natural Resources
     Geological Survey
     Water Conservation Board
     Water Resources
Department of Public Safety
     Emergency Management Agencies
Department of Revenue
State Planning and Budgeting Office

*NOTE: Names and functions of state agencies vary from state to state and this list should be adapted accordingly.

Table 4. Continued

Federal Government Users

Department of Agriculture
  Farmers' Home Administration
  Forest Service
  Soil Conservation Service
Department of the Army
  Army Corps of Engineers
Department of Commerce
  National Bureau of Standards
  National Oceanic and Atmospheric
    Agency
Department of Housing and Urban
  Development
  Federal Housing Administration
Department of the Interior
  Bureau of Land Management
  Bureau of Reclamation
  Geological Survey
  National Park Service
Department of the Navy
Department of Transportation
  Federal Highway Administration
Environmental Protection Agency
Federal Emergency Management Agency
General Services Administration
Members of Congress and their staffs
Nuclear Regulatory Commission
Small Business Administration

Private, Corporate, and Quasi-Public Users

Civic and voluntary groups
Concerned citizens, homeowners associations
Construction companies
Consulting planners, geologists, architects, and
  engineers
Economic development committees
Extractive, manufacturing, and processing
  industries
Financial and insuring institutions
Landowners, developers, and real estate agents
News media
Utility and transmission companies
University departments (including geology,
  civil engineering, architecture, urban and
  regional planning, and environmental
  studies departments)

Other National Users

Applied Technology Council
American Association of State Highway and
  Transportation Officials
American Public Works Association
American Red Cross
Association of Engineering Geologists
Association of State Geologists
Council of State Governments
Earthquake Engineering Research Institute
International Conference of Building Officials
National Academy of Sciences
National Association of Counties
National Association of Insurance
  Commissioners
National Governors' Association
National Institute of Building Sciences
Natural Hazards Research and Applications
  Information Center, University of Colorado
National League of Cities
Professional and scientific societies (including
  geologic, engineering, architecture, and
  planning societies)
United States Conference of Mayors

Most states have professional planners, engineers, or geologists available who can make interpretations from available hazard information. Specialists from the federal government who are skilled in the translation of technical data can also assist states. As suggested in Chapter 4, the most effective use of landslide information is achieved when maps are prepared that indicate the location, severity, and recurrence potential of landslides.

Developing an Information Base: Sources of Landslide Hazard Information

Some of the organizations that produce or provide landslide hazard information are listed in Table 5.

Table 5. Examples of producers and providers of landslide hazard information (adapted from U.S. Geological Survey, 1982).

American Institute of Professional Geologists
American Society of Civil Engineers
Association of Engineering Geologists
County extension agents
Educators (university, college, high school)
Museum of Natural History
State Department of Highways
State Geological Survey
Hazard researchers, interpreters, and mappers
International Conference of Building Officials
Journalists, commentators, editors, and other news professionals
Local seismic safety advisory groups
National Governors' Association
Natural Hazards Research and Applications Information Center, University of Colorado
Public information offices (federal and state)
U.S. Army Corps of Engineers
U.S. Bureau of Land Management
U.S. Bureau of Reclamation
U.S. Forest Service
U.S. Geological Survey
U.S. Soil Conservation Service

❏

Chapter 6
Landslide Loss–Reduction Techniques

A significant reduction in landslide losses can be achieved by preventing or minimizing the exposure of populations and facilities to landsliding; by preventing, reducing, or managing the actual occurrence of landslides; and by physically controlling landslide-prone slopes and protecting existing structures.

Subsidized insurance is not considered a loss-reduction technique because it does not prevent or reduce losses but merely transfers the loss to other segments of the population. Indeed, it may encourage lenders to develop hazardous lands because they are indemnified by uninvolved taxpayers. The insurance industry could become a strong promoter of hazards reduction if it would establish its rates to reflect relative risks. Most homeowners' insurance policies exclude coverage for ground movements, including landslides.

Preventing or Minimizing Exposure to Landslides

Vulnerability to landslide hazards is a function of a site's location, type of activity, and frequency of landslide events. Thus, the vulnerability of human life, activity, and property to landsliding can be lowered by total avoidance of landslide hazard areas or by restricting, prohibiting, or imposing conditions on hazard-zone activity. Local governments can accomplish this by adopting land-use regulations and policies and restricting redevelopment.

Land–Use Regulations

Land-use regulations and policies are often the most economical and effective means of regulation available to a community—particularly if enacted prior to development. However, where potentially hazardous land is privately owned with the expectation of relatively intense development and use, or where land optimally suited for development in communities is in short supply, there is strong motivation and pressure to use the land intensively. Land-use regulations must be balanced against economic considerations, political realities, and historical rights.

Various types of land-use regulations and development policies can be used to reduce landslide hazards. Some of these methods are listed in Table 2, Chapter 2. Responsibility for their implementation resides primarily with local governments, with some involvement of state and federal governments and the private sector.

Reducing the Occurrence of Landslides and Managing Landslide Events

As discussed in Chapter 3, many landslides occur as a direct result of human activities. The excavation and grading associated with the construction of buildings, highways, transmission lines, and reservoirs can create conditions that will ultimately result in slope failure. The development and enforcement of codes for excavation, grading, and construction can prevent such landslides. A review of the state of the art and standards of performance of hillside and flatland urban development from the 1950s to the early 1980s is available in a training manual (Scullin, 1982). This manual describes the mitigation of several geologic hazards: landsliding, subsidence, expansive soils, drainage, and earthquakes. The concepts and technical applications described in this book may be applied in short-or long-term planning regarding geologic risks anywhere.

Building and Grading Codes

Design, building, and grading codes are regulatory tools available to local government agencies for achieving desired design and building practices. They can be applied to both new construction and pre-existing buildings. In rare cases, such as those involving large offshore structures, the effect of landslides can be considered explicitly as part of the design, and the facility can be built to resist landslide damage. In some cases, existing structures in landslide-prone areas can be modified to be more accommodating to landslide movement. The extent to which this is successful depends on the type of landsliding to which the structure is exposed. Facilities other than buildings (e.g., gas pipelines and water mains) can also be designed to tolerate ground movement. Codes and regulations governing grading and excavation can reduce the likelihood that construction of buildings and highways will increase the degree to which a location is prone to landslides. Various codes that have been developed for federal, state, and local implementation can be used as models for landslide-damage mitigation. A fundamental concern with design and building codes is their enforcement in a uniform and equitable way. (Committee on Ground Failure Hazards, 1985, p. 15).

Emergency Management

Emergency management and emergency planning contribute to landslide loss reduction by saving lives and reducing injuries. Such planning can also protect and preserve property in those cases where property is mobile or where protective structures can be installed if sufficient warning time is available.

Emergency management and planning consist of identifying potential hazards, determining the required actions and parties responsible for implementing mitigation actions, and ensuring the readiness of necessary emergency response personnel, equipment, supplies, and facilities. An important element of emergency management is a program of public education and awareness informing citizens of their potential exposure, installation of warning systems, types of warnings to be issued, probable evacuation routes and times available, and appropriate protective actions to be taken.

A warning system may include the monitoring of geologic and meteorologic conditions (e.g., rates of landslide movement, snowmelt runoff, storm development) with potential for causing a catastrophic event or the placement of signs instructing people within a potentially hazardous area of proper procedures (Figure 24). Automatic sensors, located within land-

slide-prone areas, with effective linkages to a central communication warning facility and, thence, to individuals with disaster management responsibilities, are also sometimes used. Warning systems can be long-term or temporary—used only when high risk conditions exist or while physical mitigation methods are being designed and built (Figure 25).

Figure 24. Sign placed in some of the hazardous mountain canyon areas of Colorado.

Controlling Landslide-Prone Slopes and Protecting Existing Structures

Physical reduction of the hazard posed by unstable slopes can be undertaken in areas where human occupation already poses a risk, but where measures such as zoning are precluded by the cost of resettlement, value or scarcity of land, or historical rights. Physical measures can attempt to either control and stabilize the hazard or to protect persons and property at risk.

It is not possible, feasible, or even necessarily desirable to prevent all slope movements. Furthermore, it may not be economically feasible to undertake physical modifications in some landslide areas. Where land is scarce, however, investment in mitigation may increase land value and make more expensive and elaborate mitigation designs feasible.

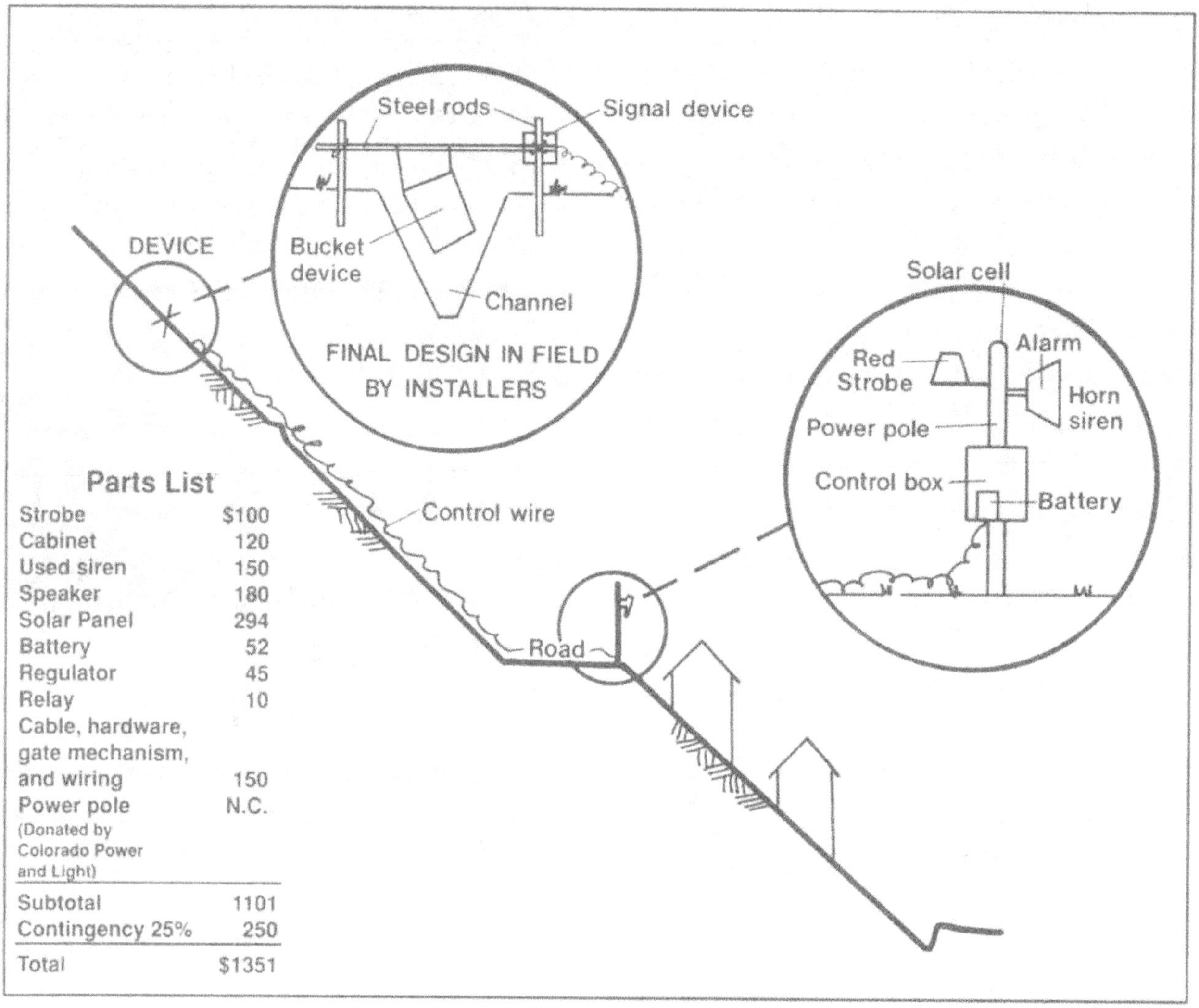

Steel rods

Signal device

DEVICE

Bucket device

Channel

FINAL DESIGN IN FIELD BY INSTALLERS

Solar cell

Red Strobe

Alarm

Power pole

Horn siren

Control box

Battery

Parts List

Strobe	$100
Cabinet	120
Used siren	150
Speaker	180
Solar Panel	294
Battery	52
Regulator	45
Relay	10
Cable, hardware, gate mechanism, and wiring	150
Power pole (Donated by Colorado Power and Light)	N.C.
Subtotal	1101
Contingency 25%	250
Total	$1351

Control wire

Road

Figure 25. Schematic of a warning system (by Robert Kistner, Kistner and Associates).

Landslide control structures can be costly and usually require considerable lead time for project planning and design, land acquisition, permitting, and construction (Figure 26). Such structures may have significant environmental and socioeconomic impacts that should be considered in planning.

Precautions Concerning Reliance on Physical Methods

Although physical techniques may be the only means for protecting existing land uses in hazard areas, sole reliance on them may create a false sense of security. An event of greater severity than that for which the project was designed may occur, or a structure may fail due to aging, changing conditions, inadequate design,

Figure 26. Rudd Creek debris basin in Farmington, Utah constructed in 1983–84 (photograph by Robert Kistner, Kistner and Associates).

or improper maintenance. The result could be catastrophic if the hazard zone has been developed intensively.

Design Considerations and Physical Mitigation Methods

When designing control measures, it is essential to look well beyond the landslide mass itself. A translational slide may propagate over great distances if the failure surface is sufficiently inclined and the shear resistance along the surface remains lower than the driving force. Debris flows can frequently be better controlled if mitigation efforts emphasize stabilizing the source area along with debris containment in the runout area. An understanding of the geological processes and the surface- and ground-water conditions, under both natural and human-imposed conditions, is essential to any mitigation planning.

Some factors that determine the choice of physical mitigation are:

- type of movement (e.g., fall, slide, avalanche, flow);
- kinds of materials involved (rock, soil, debris);
- size, location, depth of failure;
- process that initiated movement;
- people, place(s), or thing(s) affected by failure;
- potential for enlargement (certain types of failures [e.g., rotational slides, earthflows, translational slides] will enlarge during excavation);
- availability of resources (funding, labor force, materials);
- accessibility and space available for physical mitigation;
- danger to people;
- property ownership and liability.

The physical mitigation of landslides usually consists of a combination of methods. Drainage control is used most often; slope modification by cut and fill and/or buttresses is the second most frequently used method. These are also, in general, the least expensive techniques (Figure 27).

Various types of physical mitigation methods are listed in Table 6.

Figure 27. Retaining wall, Interstate 70, near Vail, Colorado (photograph by Colorado Geological Survey).

Table 6. Physical mitigation methods (Colorado Geological Survey et al., 1988).

A. Physical Mitigation Methods for Slides and Slumps
  1. Drainage
    a. Surface drainage
      1) ditches
      2) regrading
      3) surface sealing
    b. Subsurface drainage
      1) horizontal drains
      2) vertical drains/wells
      3) trench drains/interceptors, cut-off drains/counterforts
      4) drainage galleries or tunnels
      5) blanket drains
      6) electro-osmosis
      7) blasting
      8) subsurface barriers
  2. Excavation or regrading of the slope
    a. Total removal of landslide mass
    b. Regrading of the slope
    c. Excavation to unload the upper part of the landslide
    d. Excavation and replacement of the toe of the landslide with other materials
  3. Restraining structures
    a. Retaining walls
    b. Piles
    c. Buttresses and counterweight fills
    d. Tie rods and anchors

Table 6. Continued

    e. Rock bolts/anchors/dowels
4. Vegetation
5. Soil hardening
    a. Chemical treatment
    b. Freezing
    c. Thermal treatment
    d. Grouting
B. Physical Mitigation Methods for Debris Flows and Debris Avalanches
  1. Source-area stabilization
    a. Check dams
    b. Revegetation
  2. Energy dissipation and flow control
    a. Check dams
    b. Deflection walls
    c. Debris basins
    d. Debris fences
    e. Deflection dams
    f. Channelization

  3. Direct protection
    a. Impact spreading walls
    b. Stem walls
    c. Vegetation barriers
C. Physical Mitigation Methods for Rockfalls
  1. Stabilization
    a. Excavation
    b. Benching
    c. Scaling and trimming
    d. Rock bolts/anchors/dowels
    e. Chains and cables
    f. Anchored mesh nets
    g. Shotcrete
    h. Buttresses
    j. Dentition
  2. Protection
    a. Rock-trap ditches
    b. Catch nets and fences
    c. Catch walls
    d. Rock sheds or tunnels

❏

Chapter 7
Plan Preparation

Determining the Need for a State Plan

In order to determine the need for a state landslide hazard mitigation plan, individual states must first assess the vulnerability of their present and future population to the hazard. **Vulnerability** is the susceptibility or exposure to injury or loss from a hazard. People, structures, community infrastructure systems (transportation, water supply, communications, and electricity), and social systems are all potentially vulnerable.

An assessment of statewide vulnerability to geologic hazards is a product of the technical assessment of the problem, based on scientific studies and investigations, and an assessment of capabilities, in the public and private sectors, to respond to and mitigate the hazards and potential impacts identified. Before resources are invested in hazard mitigation measures, the social and economic costs and impacts associated with landsliding need to be determined and put into perspective.

The next step in recognizing the overall vulnerability of the state to the landslide hazard is the identification of specific communities, areas, and facilities at risk. The existence and effectiveness of local programs and systems for mitigating landslide problems in communities experiencing actual or potential impacts must then be determined.

Although landslides can potentially affect entire regions or states, the hazards themselves are local problems first, and local governments remain on the "front lines" of the battle to reduce losses.

> Landslide loss reduction in the United States is primarily a local responsibility. While the federal government plays a key role in research, in the development of mapping techniques, and in landslide management on federal lands, the reduction of landslide losses through land use management and the application of building and grading codes is essentially a function of local government (Sangrey and Bernstein, 1985, p. 9).

The purpose of a state landslide hazard mitigation plan is to encourage and support local mitigation efforts and address serious landslide problems, beyond local capability, that threaten lives and property and have potential regional or statewide implications. Strategies and projects developed in the planning process are therefore based on an assessment of what can be accomplished locally and the level of supplemental assistance that will be required to lessen the problem. State and federal assistance picks up where local efforts stop; generally local resources must first be exhausted.

A key element in the planning process and a major recommendation of this guidebook is the establishment of a permanent state organization, representing the various levels and responsibilities of government, to focus the attention of state government on natural hazard mitigation issues.

Federal Disaster Relief and Emergency Assistance Act (Section 409)

In presidentially-declared disasters, the preparation of a state plan that identifies and evaluates hazard mitigation opportunities is mandated by Section 409 of the Robert T. Stafford Disaster Relief and Emergency Assistance Act (Public Law 93–288, as amended) as a condition of receiving federal disaster assistance. This requirement was originally enacted in 1974 under Section 406 of the Disaster Relief Act to encourage identification, evaluation, and mitigation of hazards at the state and local government levels. The requirements of Section 409 are triggered by a major disaster or emergency declared by the President and apply to all types of declared emergencies and disasters. A hazard mitigation clause is incorporated into the FEMA/State agreement for disaster assistance, thereby establishing the identification of hazards and the evaluation of hazard mitigation opportunities as a condition for receiving federal assistance.

The Federal Emergency Management Agency (FEMA) is responsible for administering the Section 409 requirements and has prepared implementing regulations (44 CFR 206, Subpart M) that specify federal, state, and local responsibilities under Section 409. Under the regulations, a state hazard mitigation coordinator is designated by a governor's authorized representative to prepare a hazard mitigation plan and to ensure its implementation. States may establish a group of individuals from state and local agencies to assist in preparing the "409 plan," which must be completed and submitted to FEMA within 180 days after the presidential declaration.

With the passage of the Stafford Act in 1988, a hazard mitigation funding program was authorized for the first time under Section 404 of the Act. This mitigation-measures funding program provides up to 50 percent federal funding for activities identified under Section 404, thus making preparation of a good hazard mitigation plan more important than ever before. The identification of mitigation opportunities under this program follows the evaluation of natural hazards under Section 409. Total federal funds available under Section 404 are limited to 10 percent of the permanent restorative work funded under FEMA's Public Assistance Program. Implementation regulations for Section 404 can also be found in 44 CFR 206, Subpart M.

In state-declared disasters, some states require the development of local hazard mitigation plans as an eligibility requirement of state emergency relief.

The Planning Team

States undertaking plan development should first consider assembling a state planning team to manage the research and writing of the plan. The planning team could be in the form of a working group, directed by state representatives and supported by representatives of local government, the private sector, and academia. Typically, the group would gather, interpret, and assemble the technical information that forms the basic structure of the landslide hazard mitigation plan.

The interagency efforts of post-disaster hazard mitigation teams in presidentially-declared disasters have demonstrated that such working groups representing a broad range of state and federal agencies can successfully develop a host of innovative and cost-effective mitigation ideas.

The planning team should include individuals knowledgeable about geology, engineering, emergency management, and community development and planning. Depending on the nature of landslide problems, the team might also include individuals involved in natural resources management, highway construction and maintenance, state and regional planning, and others as conditions warrant.

The responsibilities of individual team members would include researching and writing those sections of the plan that relate to their area of expertise. Team members would also participate in meetings with planners, emergency managers, policy makers, and elected officials in local and state government and, to the extent possible, seek the input and participation of private industry, professional and volunteer organizations, and interested citizens. An initial analysis of existing mitigation plans and emergency management capabilities in landslide-impacted jurisdictions will enable the planning team to identify the most serious problems and to develop projects that build on efforts already in progress. This assessment of local landslide conditions and local capabilities to deal with them should identify a wide variety of practicable mitigation solutions. This will facilitate the coordination of state support and the identification of unmet local needs that can be presented for possible state action.

Local jurisdictions impacted by landslides should be encouraged to form their own local planning teams—composed of decision makers, planners, emergency managers, engineers, geologists, and officials from law enforcement, fire safety, and emergency medical services—to formulate local plans and mitigation strategies.

The Planning Process

The planning process recommended for the development of a landslide hazard mitigation plan follows a series of steps that are basic to mitigation planning:

(1) analysis of the types of landslide hazards in the state and a general assessment of the vulnerability of people and property to the state's landslide hazards;

(2) identification of specific areas of the state where landslides have the most serious or immediate potential impacts and a detailed analysis of their vulnerabilities;

(3) translation and transfer of technical information on hazards and vulnerabilities to users such as decision makers, community planners, and emergency management officials;

(4) assessment of resources and mitigation programs available in the public and private sectors to deal with the identified potential impacts;

(5) determination of local capability shortfalls and unmet needs in order to apply technical and financial assistance where it can best contribute to the reduction of future losses;

(6) formulation of goals and objectives for state and local landslide hazard mitigation plans, and the development of cost-effective mitigation projects that address identified vulnerabilities;

(7) establishment of a permanent state hazard mitigation system to prioritize and promote mitigation goals and objectives and to secure and direct funding for implementation;

(8) periodic evaluation and modification of the plan and planning process.

Step 1—Hazard Analysis

A complete hazard analysis is the result of the identification of the state's landslide hazard areas, the identification of the most vulnerable locations, and the assessment of potential impacts on people and property in vulnerable areas. Where possible, the hazard analysis should provide planners with information about hazard location, description, frequency, history, existing impacts, potential impacts, and, to the extent possible, probability of occurrence.

The use of land-use maps in conjunction with detailed maps exhibiting the extent and severity of landslide hazards in an area helps officials to determine vulnerability to landslides, mitigation priorities, and the most appropriate mitigation measures.

> Appropriate land use management, effective building and grading codes, the use of well-designed engineering techniques for landslide control and stabilization, the timely issuance of emergency warnings, and the availability of landslide insurance can significantly reduce the catastrophic effects of landslides. All of these approaches require, as a starting point, the identification of areas where landslides are either statistically likely or immediately imminent, and the representation of these hazardous locations on maps (Committee on Ground Failure Hazards, 1985, p. 2).

The planning team should assemble existing mapped landslide susceptibility data that portray the distribution of various types of landslides and the likelihood of their occurrence. The team will need maps sufficiently detailed to determine the character, location, and magnitude of landslide problems.

Step 2—Identification of Impacted Sites

Once the nature and distribution of the hazard and the vulnerability to landsliding of various communities, areas, and facilities has been determined, site-specific evaluations of the potential impacts of landsliding should be performed. Based on the hazard analysis, those sites determined to present the greatest threat to lives and property should be subject to further site analysis and mitigation planning.

Impact is the effect of a hazard event on people, buildings, and the infrastructure. The impacts of landsliding range from the inconvenience of debris cleanup to the life-threatening failure of a landslide-formed dam. The simultaneous or sequential occurrence of other hazards such as flooding or earthquakes with landsliding can produce effects that are greater or qualitatively different from those produced by landsliding alone.

Step 3—Technical Information Transfer

As discussed in Chapter 5, individuals or groups often do not take mitigative actions because they do not understand the significance of the threat, what to do to reduce it, or lack information and training on how to do it. Therefore, once landslide hazard information has been gathered, it must be communicated to planners, policy makers, emergency response personnel, and the public. Maps are one of the best methods of transferring such information. Landslide information can be used in the development, review, and approval of land-use plans, community development plans, emergency management plans, and hazard mitigation plans. In order for landslide information to be more widely incorporated into community planning and planning for landslide mitigation, the technical staff that produces the information must tailor it so that it is understandable and usable by the various parties involved in the development process. Producers of information should also ensure that potential users are aware of available data, as well as research planned or in progress. Conversely, nontechnical users of landslide information should take steps to improve their skills in interpreting and applying the information.

The difficulty of translating technical information for nontechnical users highlights the importance of retaining the services of qualified technical experts throughout the planning process. According to Fleming and Taylor (1980, p. 4), "solutions to the technical problems are only a part of the process of achieving landslide hazard reduction. The political problem of transferring the information into a governmental system to reduce hazards and damages is perhaps more formidable than the technical one."

Step 4—Capability Assessment

Capability assessment is a determination of public, private, and volunteer resources in a community that are available to support emergency management and hazard mitigation activities designed to reduce losses from a particular hazard. Resources include not only equipment, supplies, and materials, but, more importantly, people, expertise, plans, programs, and cooperative agreements with other jurisdictions and private industry. Private companies have a vested interest in the mitigation process because private losses often exceed public losses in natural disasters, and also because private firms may receive insurance benefits (lower premiums, reduced liability) for a demonstrated commitment to reducing future losses.

The assessment of local capabilities should identify the most vulnerable elements of the community, the current level of mitigation activity, the status of emergency management planning, and opportunities for state and federal mitigation assistance.

The checklist provided in Table 7 can assist local jurisdictions in preparing plans for landslide hazard mitigation and emergency management as well as assisting state planning teams in assessing local mitigation efforts.

Table 7. Types of information that should be considered in an assessment of a community's landslide hazards and capabilities (modified from Weber et al., 1983).

A. Maps
    1. Base map
    2. Landslide inventories
    3. Landslide susceptibility maps
    4. Landslide hazard maps
B. Physical (Geologic) Information
    1. Scope (boundaries of areas subject to landslides)
    2. Frequency (historical occurrences by date, location, description, and impacts)
        a. Reports
        b. Newspaper articles
        c. Eyewitness accounts
    3. Hazard characteristics
        a. Predictability
        b. Potential speed of occurrence
        c. Potential impact forces
        d. Magnitude
        e. Worst-case scenario
C. Social (Human) Information
    1. Land Use
        a. Existing (map)
        b. Future (map)
        c. Zoning (map)

Table 7. Continued

2. Population at risk
   a. Number of people/total dwelling units
   b. Variability (difference in day/night populations)
3. Property at risk (infrastructure)
   a. Use/function
   b. Assessed value
4. Economic activity at risk (commercial, industrial, tourism)
   a. Employment
   b. Gross revenues
5. Critical services and facilities at risk
   a. Access
   b. Police
   c. Fire
   d. Communications
   e. Schools
   f. Health care (hospitals, nursing homes)
   g. Utilities
   h. Emergency management facilities
   i. Transportaion
6. Aggravating influences (roads, structures, landscaping, removal of vegetation, or other land uses that contribute to landslide hazard)

D. Landslide Hazard Management Capabilities
1. Landslide hazard mitigation activities
   a. Land-use regulations
   b. Land-use plans
   c. Building and grading codes
   d. Design and location standards
   e. Development and redevelopment plans
   f. Landslide control structures
   g. Monitoring/instrumentation
   h. Acquisition and relocation projects
   i. Public utility extension guidelines
   j. Planning team formation
   k. Land exchanges
   l. Real estate disclosure requirements
   m. Lending and financing policies
   n. Additional public works
   o. Private sector involvement
   p. Special assessment districts
   q. Tax adjustments

2. Emergency management activities
   a. Warning systems
   b. Emergency plans (life-saving, evacuation, facility-specific)
   c. Public education/hazard awareness campaigns
   d. Training exercises
3. Local financial capabilities and needs
   a. Funds available
   b. Major resource shortfalls
   c. State and federal programs and grants
   d. State and federal technical assistance

By comparing local risks and possible impacts with the capability of a jurisdiction to respond to those risks, a state planning team can identify major resource deficiencies, or unmet needs, that become the basis for projects in the state plan. Unmet needs are technical and financial resource needs that exceed the capabilities of the communities at risk. In many cases, these resource shortfalls represent substantial obstacles to reducing the impacts of future landslides on people, property, and essential services.

Step 5—Determination of Unmet Local Needs

Based on the analysis of local capabilities, unmet needs that should be considered by state and federal governments are identified and a state mitigation assistance strategy is formulated. In order to determine unmet needs, specific human activities should be examined to evaluate potential impacts on public health and safety, public and private property, commerce, and the community at large. Group meetings and individual interviews can yield sufficient information to determine the most critical needs of local governments and to develop priority mitigation projects for state action. Less urgent needs can be addressed in future projects. The state planning team should also identify existing local mitigation projects so that state projects can be coordinated to support their efforts.

Step 6—Formulation of Goals and Objectives

Fundamental to a mitigation program is the establishment of a system for landslide mitigation planning and management at the state and local government levels. The establishment of a permanent state system to effect mitigation projects should be considered. This management system would help ensure that:

- existing hazardous conditions are dealt with expeditiously,
- new landslide hazards are assessed and prioritized,
- new options are developed and evaluated,
- intergovernmental and interagency technical advice and mitigative action can be coordinated,
- priorities are established for high- and moderate-risk situations that are beyond local government capability,
- decisions are made and funding obtained and spread over a period of time that is commensurate with state fiscal capabilities,
- feedback is evaluated and needed program adjustments made, and
- a systematic approach to mitigation is established.

Local Landslide Hazard Mitigation

Local jurisdictions should institute mitigation programs that coordinate landslide hazard information and mitigation needs with state government and the private sector. Local mitigation systems should effectively employ state assistance and be ready to take on new problems as solutions to old problems are found. Local mitigation plans need to be in place so that work on mitigation projects can begin as soon as funds become available.

Effective local systems are important to state planning because they provide direction for state action. A comprehensive local hazard mitigation program should be based on community consensus, developed through local planning committees with citizen support and involvement, and should conform to local goals and objectives and budget constraints. Local governments involved in landslide hazard mitigation face a number of important planning challenges, including: (a) the preparation of emergency management plans that ensure the timely warning and evacuation of people in high-risk areas; (b) the formation of local planning committees to identify unmet local needs and schedule the implementation of mitigation projects; (c) the coordination of public, private, and volunteer resources; and (d) the integration of landslide hazard information into community development plans in order to protect existing development and guide, discourage, or restrict future development in landslide-prone areas.

Local hazard mitigation and emergency planning are generally carried out separately from the basic planning of local government. Integrating hazard information into the comprehensive or master plan of a community, however, better enables a jurisdiction to guide the activities of builders, investors, and developers in areas known to be hazardous. Communities that have an adequate base of technical information about local landslide problems, and that have succeeded in applying this information to development and planning decisions, have met an important precondition to most types of mitigation. Land-use plans that consider available hazard information demonstrate to developers and to the public that public health and safety concerns are important factors in community development. According to Olshansky and Rogers (1987, p. 957), "By incorporating landslide hazard information into long-term local plans, local governments give developers advance notice of land use policies and the reasons for those policies."

Development of Mitigation Projects

The identification of areas in the state that are vulnerable to catastrophic landslide losses will enable the planning team to formulate the goals and objectives of the state plan, which may be expressed in the plan in the form of prioritized mitigation projects. With the support of the planning, technical, and policy-making staff of state and local agencies that have resources, capabilities, or statutory responsibilities relating to landslide hazard management, the planning team should be able to develop an initial group of projects.

A wide range of project ideas and opinions, representing the perspectives of planning, geology, engineering, emergency management, private industry, elected leadership, and others, should be solicited to enable the planning team to determine the cost effectiveness, feasibility, and political and social implications of each possible approach. The highest initial priority should be assigned to those projects that establish a permanent system in state government for continuous support of state hazard mitigation opportunities. A second priority should be state support to long-term mitigation programs in local government and the private sector. Another ongoing priority should be the identification of and participation in state and federal programs that can provide funding support for mitigation initiatives.

Although implementation of many recommendations may be difficult if financial resources are limited, government agencies should be encouraged to use the plan and its identified projects as a resource in formulating annual work programs, budgets, and policy statements concerning landslides. Projects that modify existing programs or improve coordination are usually relatively low-cost and stand the best chance of being implemented first. Funds to implement the more costly projects should be aggressively sought from state legislatures, the federal government, and the private sector.

Projects recommended in the state plan should include a brief statement of the problem, a general statement of the recommended solution, a description of short- and long-term initiatives, a designated lead agency, and a preliminary estimate of cost effectiveness, where possible. Projects should contribute toward an effective and coordinated state/local landslide management system, and should be flexible both in content and priority to allow for modification during the implementation process. Local jurisdictions should report their accomplishments and important unmet needs to the state mitigation organization so that new state/local strategies can be developed. New projects should be introduced into the system as new landslide threats are identified and as new approaches to old problems are found.

Step 7—Establishment of a Permanent State Hazard Mitigation Organization

A permanent state hazard mitigation organization should be created to coordinate the resources of state, local, and federal agencies with landslide hazard mitigation responsibilities and authorities. For states with serious landslide problems, establishment of a permanent organization institutionalizes in state government the consideration of opportunities to reduce landslide losses. In Colorado, this has been accomplished by an Executive Order (Figure 28) that formalizes landslide hazard mitigation planning within a natural hazards mitigation council.

States with no existing system for hazard mitigation should consider establishing an organization that also addresses and promotes the mitigation of other hazards impacting the state. Most of the public agencies involved in landslide hazard mitigation—those concerned with geology, natural resources, highways, climatology, water resources, emergency management, and others—are also involved with problems of flooding, drought, and, depending upon location, hurricanes, and earthquakes. Although the focus and extent of short-term mitigation activities at any given time may depend upon the prevailing threats, the organization should maintain a broader, long-term perspective on all of a state's natural hazards. An all-hazards approach should result in an efficient, multi-purpose process that can gain the support and approval of state leadership and the public.

The role of the state mitigation organization should essentially be a continuation of the activities performed by the state planning team and those coordinating agencies with a role in landslide mitigation that participated in the development of the plan. One type of organization might consist of a state mitigation council supported by working groups. The council would be made up of decision makers selected from key state, local, and federal agencies and could include representatives from the governor's office and the state legislature. Representatives from local and regional governments and academia may also be included in working groups.

STATE OF COLORADO

EXECUTIVE CHAMBERS
136 State Capitol
Denver, Colorado 80203-1792
Phone (303) 866-2471

Roy Romer
Governor

B 044 89

EXECUTIVE ORDER

ESTABLISHING A COUNCIL FOR THE IMPLEMENTATION OF
STRATEGIES TO MANAGE MITIGATION OF NATURAL HAZARDS IN COLORADO

WHEREAS, various natural hazards have caused physical and financial impacts in Colorado and will continue to do so; and

WHEREAS, these impacts have resulted in unexpected costs to state and local governments as well as degradation of the state's health, safety, environment, infrastructure and economy; and

WHEREAS, the opportunities to significantly manage floods, landslides, wildfires and other natural hazards are identifiable and should be executed as funding is available; and

WHEREAS, mitigation recommendations can be effectively prioritized and managed by a state council, supported by interagency working groups; and

WHEREAS, a need exists to provide formal recognition, authority and responsibilities to this organizational structure;

NOW, THEREFORE, I, Roy Romer, Governor of the State of Colorado, by virtue of the authority vested in me under the constitution and laws of the State of Colorado, including the Colorado Disaster Emergency Act of 1973, 24-33.5-701, et seq., hereby Order:

1. The Colorado Natural Hazards Mitigation Council is hereby created. The council will be chaired by the Colorado Department of Natural Resources and consist of as many as 25 representatives. The following organizations or groups shall be appointed by the Governor:

- The Governor's Office
- State departments of Natural Resources, Highways, Local Affairs, Public Safety, Health and Agriculture
- The Colorado Municipal League and Colorado Counties, Inc.
- The Natural Hazards Center, University of Colorado
- Business community
- The Federal Emergency Management Agency (Region VIII) and the National Weather Service (National Oceanic and Atmospheric Administration)
- U.S. Army Corps of Engineers
- Elected local officials from areas of the state with high-risk natural hazards
- The general public

Executive Order
Page Two

B 044 89

The Speaker of the House of Representatives, the President of the Senate, the Minority Leader of the Senate and the Minority Leader of the House of Representatives may each appoint one legislative representative. All members will serve for a term of two years with reappointments permitted at the pleasure of the Governor. The Governor will appoint the chairperson.

2. The chairperson will appoint a steering committee and an executive secretary to carry on the administrative activities of the council.

3. The responsibilities assigned to the council are to:

a. Identify vulnerability to various natural hazards and evaluate the options available to mitigate such risks.

b. Review current mitigation plans for such hazards as wildfires, droughts and avalanches.

c. Develop a unified management strategy with recommendations concerning state, federal or local mitigation responsibilities.

d. Prioritize hazards statewide.

e. Assist local government in seeking funding to implement hazard mitigation recommendations.

f. Meet at the call of the chairperson, but no less frequently than once a year.

g. Prepare an annual work program and status report covering progress achieved and provide periodic updates to the Governor and the state legislature.

h. Inform local government and the general public of the activities and recommendations of the council.

The council is directed to place high priority on use of the Colorado Flood Hazard Mitigation Plan and Landslide Hazard Mitigation Plan, and should coordinate and prioritize the projects contained in these plans and any other plans dealing with natural hazards.

Given under my hand and the Executive Seal of the State of Colorado, this 23rd day of March, 1989.

Roy Romer
Governor

Figure 28. Executive Order establishing Colorado Natural Hazards Mitigation Council.

The council should be responsible for prioritizing strategies and projects, securing and directing funding, and monitoring overall program effectiveness to ensure that policies and directed measures are implemented in a timely and efficient fashion. Since funds for the implementation of many of the recommended projects will not likely be immediately available, an ongoing and aggressive search for funding sources will be a major role of the council. State and federal support should be obtained immediately for those projects that address landslides where potentially catastrophic or serious economic impacts have been identified.

The responsibilities of the working groups will be to: (1) review risks and options and provide additional information to the council once projects have been selected from the plan for implementation, (2) monitor identified landslide areas and collect and interpret information about emergency situations as they occur, (3) prepare new projects as needed to meet changing conditions, (4) implement projects as funding becomes available, (5) recommend projects for funding by government and the private sector as specific needs arise, and (6) provide technical support to the council, including recommendations on project priority.

Step 8—Review and Revision

A continuous process for evaluating mitigation progress and for making adjustments to the program should be a part of any hazard mitigation system. Procedures for review and revision of plans and the planning process are discussed in the following chapter. ❏

Chapter 8
Review and Revision of the Plan and the Planning Process

In order to ensure the timely implementation of mitigation projects recommended in the state landslide mitigation plan, the proposed state hazard mitigation organization will need to establish an ongoing system for evaluation and modification of the planning process. In addition to tracking progress of the program and providing a record of local and state mitigation achievements, a review process permits the adjustment of program priorities. It allows the state mitigation organization to monitor and become familiar with the types of problems that are likely to be encountered in future projects, so that planning strategies can be developed.

> The criteria, decisions, and methods used in applying the landslide research findings to planning and decision making can be of value to other jurisdictions in which similar hazards exist, and for which adequate landslide information is available. The adaption to, and adoption by, other jurisdictions depends upon the presence of similar public awareness, enabling legislation, hazard issues, priorities, community interest, innovative decision makers, and staff capabilities (U.S. Geological Survey, 1982, p. 44).

While the exact nature of the evaluation system should be determined by the mitigation organization in each state based on specific needs, it is recommended that any system for evaluating the success of state landslide hazard mitigation programs include the following components:

- an inventory of landslide costs,
- an evaluation of mitigation projects and techniques,
- cost-benefit analyses of local mitigation programs.

Inventory of Landslide Costs

An effort should be made to document all landslide-related losses in the state as they occur, particularly direct damage to roads and high-ways, homes and businesses, and facilities and services, so that decisions can be made regarding the level of mitigation assistance required to reduce losses in an area and so that the cost-effectiveness of individual projects can be determined. The inventory should provide a summary of landslide incidents and associated financial impacts on individuals, companies, municipalities, and local, state, and federal governments. The inventory should include a list of occurrences, the location, type of event, cause of event, facilities damaged, total costs of damages and/or repair and replacement, and maps and photographs of affected areas. To the extent possible, an estimate of indirect damages should also be made.

> Understanding the cost and significance of natural disasters allows officials at all levels of government to make decisions about how much money should be allocated to disaster prevention rather than to the repair of damaged facilities and disaster relief after an event (Fleming and Taylor, 1980 p. 1).

Evaluation of Mitigation Projects and Techniques

The state hazard mitigation organization should establish procedures for the periodic review and evaluation of the status of individual mitigation projects, those proposed, completed, and in progress. The effectiveness of landslide hazard mitigation efforts varies according to the physical, economic, and political conditions existing in the local areas. According to Kockelman (1986, p. 47), "Very few systematic evaluations have been made of hazard-reduction techniques, even fewer for landslides specifically." A careful assessment of the cost effectiveness of each project will help guide decisions of the state hazard mitigation organization about the implementation of future projects.

The occurrence of actual landslide disasters and the identification of new landslide threats will also necessitate an adjustment of planning priorities. Maintaining flexibility in the system will enable the state organization to apply limited funds and resources to efforts that are most likely to contribute to the reduction of future losses.

Examples of Innovative Mitigation Approaches

The evaluation process will produce a record of both mitigation achievements and failures, each of which will help educate officials involved in solving landslide problems. Examples of innovative mitigation techniques that have been successfully implemented are not only of value as guidance in other jurisdictions, but will also provide justification for gaining funds and support for new projects. Additionally, promoting mitigation success stories increases public education and awareness of landslide hazards, as well as public confidence in government hazard mitigation programs.

Analyses of Local Mitigation Programs

A critical feature of the proposed planning process is the development and maintenance of lines of communication between local and state mitigation systems and between state and federal systems. In order for state mitigation assistance to adequately support local efforts, local programs must periodically report to the state their unmet needs, i.e., desired projects that are determined locally to be needed, but are beyond local resource capabilities.

Local reports of mitigation needs and activities in progress will help state officials determine program effectiveness and funding priorities. Landslides that present potentially catastrophic impacts and local mitigation programs that have demonstrated the ability to produce mitigation results should be among the top priorities considered for state or federal assistance. ❏

Chapter 9
Approaches for Overcoming Anticipated Problems

The process of developing and implementing long-term state and local landslide hazard mitigation programs is beset with certain obstacles to success. The most significant problem is generating the resolve and motivation to organize, implement, and fund such a broad-scale effort. The expenditure of the time and money necessary to derive long-term benefits is not always attractive to state or local leaders. Unfortunately, sometimes only an actual disaster will provoke action. Developing creative approaches to financing and obtaining leadership support for mitigation projects is an ongoing challenge to mitigation proponents. Nevertheless, it is clear that the ultimate costs to taxpayers are likely to be significantly increased when mitigation activities are postponed.

Organizational Problems

The need for the plan preparation team and subsequent permanent hazard mitigation organization to be broadly representative, multidisciplinary, and intergovernmental presents some immediate organizational and coordination problems. An important first step in organizing such a group is to ensure that all elements of the team concur with their roles and assignments before work begins. This agreement should be formalized in a contract, memorandum of understanding, or some other document. A further recommendation is that a project manager be appointed early on to schedule meetings, tend to administrative and financial details, ensure deadlines are met, and direct and coordinate the effort.

The project manager should be selected from the state organization designated as the lead agency and one of his or her first tasks is to integrate the broad range of technical, planning, community, and organizational expertise available into an effective working team. Elim-inating jargon and arriving at acceptable terminology for planning may require some compromise among team members. On-site visits to selected landslide areas within the state and the collection of pertinent reports and literature are important steps that the planning team should undertake. It may also be useful to organize a technical advisory committee that would meet occasionally to review draft plan material and to provide overall guidance and recommendations.

Management Problems

The research and writing efforts involved in creating a state plan will involve geologists, engineers, planners, emergency managers, elected officials, and interested citizens. The integration of these many points of view is a difficult management task but necessary if the plan is to be practical and usable for the management and mitigation of landslide hazards. The project manager, with guidance and help from other members of the team, must manage this work and establish tasks, assignments, and completion dates. In order to obtain a clear and consistent document, an editor with some background in natural hazards, earth sciences, planning and/or mitigation technology should be employed.

Financial Problems

Regardless of the source or sources of funding for development of the plan, careful management of a budget will be required to ensure all project expenses are accommodated (staff costs, travel expenses, fees for editing, printing, graphics, etc.). Since the planning process will involve several agencies working on independent tasks, periodic reviews of the budget should be conducted to prevent overruns.

Coordination Problems

Because of the difficulty involved in managing such a comprehensive effort, it is important to set realistic deadlines and to allow sufficient time for necessary coordination of involved agencies and integration of the various work elements. The involvement of all levels of government will necessarily affect progress in plan preparation, and time must be allowed for obtaining concurrence and approval from governmental agencies contributing to the mitigation process. In addition, executive and/or legislative leadership that will formally approve the plan should be kept informed of the work and made aware of the plan well in advance of publication.

Finally, in order to produce a single, clear draft of the plan, it is also necessary to coordinate the word processing systems of the participating agencies. If compatibility between computer systems is not possible, the various elements of the plan may have to be re-entered into one system. The time and expense of plan publication (typesetting, printing, distribution) should also be determined as soon as possible to permit identification of realistic deadlines. ❑

References Cited

Advisory Board on the Built Environment, 1983, *Multiple hazard mitigation strategies for communities prone to multiple natural hazards*: National Research Council, National Academy Press, Washington, D.C., 60 pp.

Advisory Committee on the International Decade for Natural Hazard Reduction, 1987, *Confronting natural disasters*: National Research Council, U.S. National Academy of Sciences, and U.S. National Academy of Engineering, National Academy Press, Washington, D.C., 60 pp.

Allen, P.M., and Flanigan, W.D., 1986, *Geology of Dallas, Texas, United States of America*: Bulletin of the Association of Engineering Geologists, v. 23, no. 4, pp. 363–418.

Alfors, J.T., Burnett, J.L., and Gay, T.E., 1973, *Urban geology master plan for California—the nature, magnitude and costs of geologic hazards in California and recommendations for their mitigation*: Bulletin 198, California Division of Mines and Geology, Sacramento, California, 112 pp.

Bernknopf, R.L., Brookshire, D.S., Campbell, R.H., Shapiro, C.D., and Fleming, R.W., 1985, The economics of landslide mitigation strategies in Cincinnati, Ohio: A methodology for benefit-cost analysis: Chapter D, **in** *Feasibility of a nationwide program for the identification and delineation of hazards from mud flows and other landslides*: Open File Report 85–276D, U.S. Geological Survey, Reston, Virginia, 16 pp.

Brabb, E.E., 1984a, *Minimum landslide damage in the United States, 1973–1983*: Open-File Report 84–486, U.S. Geological Survey, Reston, Virginia 8 pp.

———, 1984b, Innovative approaches to landslide hazard and risk mapping, **in** *Proceedings of the 4th International Symposium on Landslides*, Toronto, Canada, September 1984, v. 1, pp. 307–323.

Briggs, R.P., Pomeroy, J.S., and Davies, W.E., 1975, *Landsliding in Allegheny County, Pennsylvania*: Circular 728, U.S. Geological Survey, Reston, Virginia, 18 pp.

Colorado Geological Survey, Colorado Division of Disaster Emergency Services, and University of Colorado Center for Community Development and Design, 1988, *Colorado landslide hazard mitigation plan*: Bulletin 48, Colorado Geological Survey, Denver, Colorado, 149 pp.

Colorado Water Conservation Board and Colorado Division of Disaster Emergency Services, 1985, *Flood hazard mitigation plan for Colorado*: Colorado Water Conservation Board, Denver, Colorado, 234 pp.

Colton, R.B., Holligan, J.A., Anderson, L.W., and Patterson, P.E., 1975, *Preliminary map of landslide deposits, Durango 1° x 2° Quadrangle, Colorado*: Map MF–703 U.S. Geological Survey, Reston, Virginia.

Committee on Ground Failure Hazards, 1985a, *Reducing losses from landsliding in the United States*: National Research Council, Commission on Engineering and Technical Systems, National Academy Press, Washington, D.C., 41 pp.

Eisbacher, G.H., and Clague, J.J., 1984, *Destructive mass movements in high mountains—hazard and management*: Paper 84–16, Geological Survey of Canada, Ottawa, Canada, 230 pp.

Ellen, S.D., and Mark, R.K., 1988, *Automated modeling of debris-flow hazard using digital elevation models*: EOS Transactions of the American Geophysical Union, v. 69, no. 16, 347 pp..

Erley, D., and Kockelman, W.J., 1981, *Reducing landslide hazards—a guide for planners*: Planning Advisory Service Report no. 359, American Planning Association, 29 pp.

Filson, J.R., 1987, *Geological hazards programs and research in the U.S.A.*: Episodes, v. 10, no. 4, pp. 292–295.

Fleming, R.W., and Taylor, F.A., 1980, *Estimating the costs of landslide damage in the United States*: Circular 832, U.S. Geological Survey, Reston, Virginia, 21 pp.

Gray, R.E. and Gardner, G.D., 1977, *Processes of colluvial slope development of McMechen, West Virginia*: Bulletin of the International Association of Engineering Geology, no. 16, pp. 29–32.

Kaliser B.N. and Slosson, J.E., 1988, *Geologic consequences of the 1983 wet year in Utah*: Miscellaneous Report 88–3, Utah Geological and Mineral Survey, Salt Lake City, Utah.

Keefer, D.K., Wilson, R.C., Mark, R.K., Brabb, E.E., Brown, W.M. III, Ellen, S.D., Harp, E.L., Wieczorek, G.F., Alger, C.S., and Zatkin, R.S., 1987, *Real-time landslide warning during heavy rainfall*: Science, v. 238, pp. 921–925.

Kockelman, W.J., 1986, *Some techniques for reducing landslide hazards:* Bulletin of the Association of Engineering Geologists, v. 23, no. 1, pp. 29–52.

Krohn, J.P., and Slosson, J.E., 1976, *Landslide Potential in the United States*: California Geology, October, 1976, pp. 224–231.

Leighton, F.B., 1976, Urban landslides: targets for land-use planning in California, **in** Coates, D.R., ed., *Urban Geomorphology*: Special Paper 174, Geological Society of America, Boulder, Colorado, pp. 37–60.

Lessing, P., Kulander, B.R., Wilson, B.D., Dean, S.L., and Woodring, S.M., 1976, *West Virginia landslides and slide-prone areas*: West Virginia Geological Survey, Environmental Geology Bulletin 15, 64 pp.

Miller, R.D., 1973, *Map showing relative slope stability in part of west-central King County, Washington*: Miscellaneous Geologic Investigations Map I–852A, U.S. Geological Survey, Washington, D.C.

Ministry of Construction (Japan), 1983, *Reference manual on erosion control works [in Japanese]*: Erosion Control Department, Tokyo, Japan, 386 pp.

Nilsen, T.H., and Turner, B.L., 1975, *Influence of rainfall and ancient landslide deposits on recent landslides (1950–71) in urban areas of Contra Costa County, California*: Bulletin 1388, U.S. Geological Survey, Reston, Virginia, 18 pp.

Olshansky, R.B., and Rogers, J.D., 1987, *Unstable ground: landslide policy in the United States*: Ecology Law Quarterly, v. 13, no. 4, pp. 939–1006.

Rogers, W.P., Ladwig, L.R., Hornbaker, A.L., Schwochow, S.D., Hart, S.S., Shelton, D.C., Scroggs, D.L., and Soule, J.M., 1974, *Guidelines and criteria for identification and land-use controls of geologic hazard and mineral resource areas*: Special Publication 6, Colorado Geological Survey, Denver, Colorado, 146 pp.

Sangrey, D.A. and Bernstein, A.B., 1985, *Landsliding—a hazard that can be mitigated*: Ground Failure, no. 1, Winter 1984–85, pp. 6–10.

Schuster, R.L., and Fleming, R.W., 1986, *Economic losses and fatalities due to landslides*: Bulletin of the Association of Engineering Geologists, v. 23, no. 1, pp. 11–28.

Scullin, C.M., 1982, *Excavation and grading code administration, inspection and enforcement*: Prentice-Hall, Englewood Cliffs, New Jersey, 405 pp.

Slosson, J.E., 1969, *The role of engineering geology in urban planning*: The Governor's Conference on Environmental Geology: Special Publication 1, Colorado Geological Survey, Denver, Colorado, pp. 8–15.

Slosson, J.E., and Krohn, J.P., 1982, Southern California landslides of 1978 and 1980, **in** *Storms, Floods and Debris Flows in Southern California and Arizona, 1978 and 1980: Proceedings of a Symposium*: National Academy Press, Washington, D.C., pp. 291–319.

University of Utah, Bureau of Economic and Business Research; Utah Department of Community and Economic Development; and Utah Office of Planning and Budget, 1984, *Flooding and Landslides in Utah—an economic impact analysis*: University of Utah, Bureau of Economic and Business Research, Salt Lake City, Utah 123 pp.

U.S. Geological Survey, 1981a, *Facing geologic and hydrologic hazards–earth sciences considerations*: Professional Paper 1240B, U.S. Geological Survey, Reston, Virginia, 108 pp.

———, 1981b, *The 1980 eruptions of Mount St. Helens, Washington*, edited by Lipman, P.W., Mullineaux, D.R., Professional Paper 1250, U.S. Geological Survey, Reston, Virginia, 844 pp.

———, 1982, *Goals and tasks of the landslide part of a ground-failure hazards-reduction program*: Circular 880, U.S. Geological Survey, Reston, Virginia, 48 pp.

Varnes, D.J., 1978, Slope movement types and processes **in** Schuster, R.L. and Krizek, R.J., eds., *Landslides—Analysis and Control*: Special Report 176, Transportation Research Board, National Academy of Sciences, Washington, D.C., pp. 11–33.

Varnes, D.J., and the International Association of Engineering Geology Commission on Landslides and Other Mass Movements on Slopes, 1984, *Landslide hazard zonation— a review of principles and practice*, in Natural Hazards, v. 3, 63 pp.

Watters, R.J., 1988, *Slide Mountain, Nevada: a landslide-induced, water flood-debris flow*: Ground Failure, no.4, Spring 1988, pp 18–19.

Weber, G., von Schulez, W., and Czerniak, R., 1983, *Flood hazard management plan for the Sheridan watershed area: Sheridan, Wyoming*: Geographic Applications and Research Group, Boulder, Colorado, 113 pp.

Wieczorek, G.F., 1982, *Map showing recently active and dormant landslides near La Honda, Central Santa Cruz Mountains, California*: Miscellaneous Field Studies Map MF–1422, U.S. Geological Survey, Reston, Virginia.

———, 1984, *Preparing a detailed landslide-inventory map for hazard evaluation and reduction*: Bulletin of the Association of Engineering Geologists, v. 21, no. 3, pp. 337–342.

Wieczorek, G.F., Wilson, R.C., and Harp, E.L., 1985, *Map showing slope stability during earthquakes in San Mateo County, California*: Miscellaneous Investigations Series Map I–1257E, U.S. Geological Survey, Reston, Virginia.

Wiggins, J.H., Slosson, J.E., and Krohn, J.P., 1978, *National hazards—earthquake, landslide, expansive soil loss models*: Techincal Report, J.H. Wiggins Company Redondo Beach, California, 162 pp.

Youd, T.L., 1978, *Major cause of earthquake damage is ground failure*: Civil Engineering, v. 48, no. 4, pp. 47–51. ❏

☆U.S. GOVERNMENT PRINTING OFFICE: 1998 -- 617 - 998 / 90567